Southern California Travel Guide 2023

Sun, Surf and Soul: Unveiling The Essence of Southern California

Garrett Patton

More Books From This Author

Japan Travel Guide 2023

Morocco Travel Guide 2023

New Zealand Travel Guide 2023

Mexico Travel and Adventure Guide

India Travel Guide 2023

Paris Travel and Adventure Guide

Santorini Travel Guide

Florence Travel Guide 2023

Dominican Republic Travel Guide

Sri Lanka Travel Guide

South Africa Travel Guide 2023

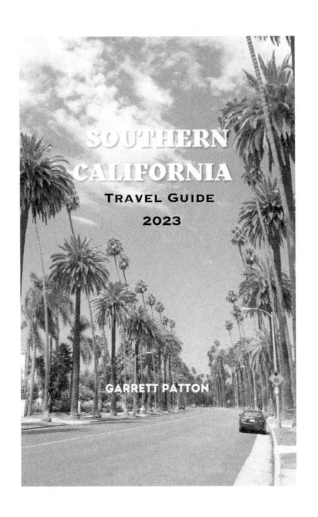

SOUTHERN CALIFORNIA

TRAVEL GUIDE

2023

GARRETT PATTON

If you have issues with any of the contents of this book or you have questions, I'll be glad to help you.

You can reach me on this email below.

Travelwithgarret62@gmail.com

Table Of Contents

Introduction To Southern California

Once upon a time, in the radiant land of Southern California, I embarked on an unforgettable adventure. The sun-kissed shores, vibrant cities, and the promise of endless possibilities drew me in like a siren's call. As I set foot in this captivating region for the very first time, I knew that my journey would be filled with incredible moments and memories that would last a lifetime.

My adventure began in Los Angeles, a city that epitomizes the glitz and glamour of the entertainment industry. Walking along the iconic Hollywood Walk of Fame, I felt a sense of awe as I gazed upon the stars, forever immortalizing the legends who had graced the silver screen. The bustling streets of downtown Los Angeles pulsated with energy, a melting pot of cultures and a testament to the city's diversity.

Eager to experience the natural beauty that Southern California had to offer, I ventured to the breathtaking coastline. The Pacific Ocean stretched out before me, its vastness both humbling and awe-inspiring. The crashing waves serenaded me as I strolled along the sun-drenched beaches of Santa Monica and Venice, feeling the warm sand between my toes. Surfers rode the crests of the waves, effortlessly gliding across the water like graceful dancers.

No trip to Southern California would be complete without a visit to San Diego, a city known for its laid-back atmosphere and stunning attractions. As I explored the historic Gaslamp Quarter, the Victorian-style buildings and vibrant nightlife transported me back in time. The San Diego Zoo was a sanctuary of biodiversity, where I marveled at the majestic elephants, playful pandas, and colorful array of exotic birds.

My journey took me further south, where I discovered the charm of Orange County. The world-famous Disneyland Resort welcomed me with open arms, and I stepped into a world of enchantment and childhood dreams. From the exhilarating rides to meeting beloved characters, I was immersed in a world of pure magic. In the coastal town of Laguna Beach, I witnessed a masterpiece of nature as the setting sun painted the sky in vibrant hues of orange and pink, casting a spell on all who beheld it.

Leaving the coast behind, I ventured into the arid desert landscapes of Palm Springs. The rugged mountains stood as sentinels, guarding the quaint oasis below. I indulged in the luxury of rejuvenating spas and basked in the tranquility of the natural hot springs. The Coachella Valley's vibrant art scene captivated me, as I explored eclectic galleries and marveled at the striking desert sculptures that seemed to defy gravity.

As my time in Southern California drew to a close, I reflected on the myriad of experiences that had touched my heart and soul. From the glitz and glamour of Los Angeles to the serene beauty of the beaches, the region had woven a tapestry of memories that would forever be etched in my mind.

Southern California had cast its spell on me, revealing its diverse tapestry of landscapes, cultures, and endless adventures. It was a place where dreams came alive, where the golden sunsets ignited the sky, and where the spirit of exploration thrived. As I bid farewell to this captivating region, I carried with me a sense of wanderlust and a newfound appreciation for the magic that resides in every corner of the world. Southern California had welcomed me as a tourist, but it had transformed me into a storyteller, ready to share the tale of my unforgettable journey with the world.

Chapter 1: Welcome To Southern California

Brief History Of Southern California

The history of Southern California is a captivating tapestry that weaves together diverse cultures, dramatic landscapes, and a relentless pursuit of the American dream. From the indigenous peoples who inhabited the region for thousands of years, to the Spanish explorers who first set foot on its shores, to the modern metropolises that now define the area, Southern California's story is one of resilience, innovation, and transformation.

The earliest known inhabitants of Southern California were the indigenous peoples, including the Tongva, Chumash, and Cahuilla tribes. These Native American communities lived in harmony with the land, developing intricate social structures, rich cultural traditions, and sustainable methods of agriculture. They thrived in the region's mild climate, abundant resources, and diverse ecosystems, leaving behind a legacy of ancient rock art, ceremonial sites, and village settlements.

The arrival of European explorers forever altered the course of Southern California's history. In 1542, Juan Rodriguez Cabrillo, a Portuguese navigator sailing under the Spanish flag, became the first recorded European to explore the region. He landed in present-day San Diego and claimed the land for Spain. Despite initial Spanish interest, it was not until the late 18th century that colonization efforts gained momentum.

In 1769, Gaspar de Portolá, a Spanish soldier, led an expedition to establish missions and presidios along the California coast. The most famous of these missions was the Mission San Juan Capistrano, founded in 1776. These missions were part of Spain's broader plan to extend their influence in the New World and convert Native Americans to Christianity. The Franciscan friars who oversaw the missions introduced European farming techniques, livestock, and new crops, forever altering the landscape and culture of the region.

In 1821, Mexico gained independence from Spain, leading to a shift in power in California. The Mexican government secularized the missions, stripping them of their religious functions and redistributing the land. This resulted in vast land grants, or ranchos, being awarded to prominent Mexican citizens. Ranchos such as Rancho Los Cerritos, Rancho

Santa Anita, and Rancho San Pedro became centers of agriculture and trade, shaping the development of the region.

The history of Southern California took a dramatic turn in 1848 with the signing of the Treaty of Guadalupe Hidalgo, which ended the Mexican-American War. Under the terms of the treaty, Mexico ceded California to the United States. The discovery of gold in the Sierra Nevada foothills that same year further fueled the region's rapid growth. The California Gold Rush drew thousands of fortune seekers to the area, transforming small towns into bustling cities virtually overnight.

The completion of the First Transcontinental Railroad in 1869 solidified Southern California's position as a vital transportation hub and opened the region to even greater waves of migration. People from all walks of life flocked to the region, seeking opportunities in agriculture, oil exploration, and the burgeoning film industry. Los Angeles, in particular, emerged as a cultural and economic powerhouse, attracting visionaries, entrepreneurs, and dreamers.

The early 20th century witnessed the birth of the entertainment industry in Southern California. Hollywood became the epicenter of the American film industry, with studios like Paramount Pictures, Warner Bros., and Universal Pictures establishing themselves in the region. The rise of Hollywood brought fame, glamour, and economic prosperity, forever shaping the identity of Southern California.

The region also played a pivotal role in World War II. Southern California became a major manufacturing center, producing aircraft, munitions, and ships to support the war effort. The influx of defense industries and military personnel led to a population boom and the development of suburbs to accommodate the growing workforce.

Following the war, Southern California experienced unprecedented growth and urbanization. The advent of the automobile and the construction of an extensive highway system facilitated suburban expansion and the development of sprawling communities. The post-war era also saw the rise of aerospace and technology industries, with companies like Lockheed Martin, Northrop Grumman, and IBM establishing a presence in the region. Southern California became a hub of innovation, attracting skilled professionals and further fueling economic growth.

The region's diverse population continued to evolve and contribute to its vibrant cultural fabric. Waves of immigration from Mexico, Asia, Europe, and other parts of the United States brought new traditions, languages, and perspectives to Southern California. This cultural diversity is evident in the region's cuisine, arts, music, and celebrations, creating a melting pot of different influences that enriches the social landscape.

Environmental consciousness and preservation efforts have also played a significant role in the history of Southern California. The region's stunning natural beauty, including its picturesque beaches, majestic mountains, and lush forests, has long been a source of inspiration and a sanctuary for residents and visitors alike. Preservation movements emerged to protect these cherished landscapes, leading to the establishment of national parks, state parks, and conservation areas. Today, millions of people enjoy outdoor activities such as hiking, surfing, and skiing, making Southern California a paradise for outdoor enthusiasts.

However, the history of Southern California also includes moments of struggle and adversity. The region has faced challenges such as devastating earthquakes, droughts, and wildfires that have tested the resilience of its communities. The construction of infrastructure, such as dams and aqueducts, was necessary to provide water to support the growing population, but it also had environmental and social implications.

Balancing the demands of development with sustainable practices and environmental stewardship continues to be an ongoing challenge for the region.

In recent decades, Southern California has become a global leader in technology, entertainment, and innovation. The Silicon Beach area in Los Angeles has become a thriving hub for startups and tech companies, while renowned universities and research institutions continue to drive scientific and technological advancements. The entertainment industry remains a major force, producing blockbuster films, acclaimed television series, and influential music.

Southern California's history is a testament to the spirit of exploration, resilience, and ambition that has defined the American West. It is a story of diverse cultures coming together, of dreams being realized, and of constant reinvention. From the indigenous peoples who first called this land home to the millions who now inhabit its bustling cities, Southern California remains a place where dreams are pursued, where innovation thrives, and where the allure of a better future continues to shape its vibrant history.

Climate and Geography

Southern California, a region renowned for its idyllic beaches, vibrant cities, and stunning natural beauty, boasts a climate and geography that have captured the hearts of many. From the sun-drenched coastline to the rugged mountains and vast deserts, this area is a fascinating tapestry of diverse landscapes and unique ecosystems. In this detailed exploration, we delve into the captivating climate patterns and geographical features that define Southern California.

Geography

Southern California is located on the southwestern coast of the United States and encompasses a vast area that spans several counties, including Los Angeles, San Diego, Orange, Riverside, and San Bernardino. The region is a blend of coastal plains, mountains, valleys, and deserts, offering a remarkable range of geographical features to explore.

Coastal Plains: The western edge of Southern California is lined with picturesque coastal plains that stretch from Santa Barbara in the north to San Diego in the south. These low-lying areas are characterized by sandy beaches, coastal cliffs, and fertile valleys that support agriculture, particularly in areas like the Oxnard Plain and the Santa Maria Valley.

Transverse Ranges: Running parallel to the coast, the Transverse Ranges dominate the region's geography. This mountain range comprises several subranges, including the Santa Monica Mountains, San Gabriel Mountains, San Bernardino Mountains, and Santa Ana Mountains. These rugged peaks, some reaching over 10,000 feet (3,000 meters), offer breathtaking vistas, extensive hiking trails, and a wealth of outdoor recreational opportunities.

Inland Valleys: Nestled between the Transverse Ranges and the Coast Ranges lies a series of fertile inland valleys. The most prominent of these is the Central Valley, which stretches north of Los Angeles, providing ample agricultural land for farming activities. These valleys are characterized by moderate temperatures, fertile soils, and lush vegetation, making them ideal for farming and viticulture.

Mojave and Colorado Deserts: Eastern Southern California is home to two distinct desert regions—the Mojave Desert in the north and the Colorado Desert in the south. The Mojave Desert is known for its iconic Joshua trees, vast expanses of sand dunes, and stunning rock formations, including the famous Joshua Tree National Park. The Colorado Desert, a part of the larger Sonoran Desert, features unique desert ecosystems, including the beautiful Anza-Borrego Desert State Park.

Climate
Southern California experiences a Mediterranean climate with mild, wet winters and warm, dry summers. However, due to its vast size and

diverse topography, there are variations in climate across the region.

Coastal Climate: The coastal areas of Southern California are influenced by the cool California Current, which brings cold water from the north. This results in a maritime climate characterized by mild, relatively stable temperatures throughout the year. Summers are warm and dry, with average temperatures ranging from the mid-70s to mid-80s Fahrenheit (24-29 degrees Celsius). Winters are mild and wet, with average temperatures ranging from the mid-50s to low 60s Fahrenheit (12-16 degrees Celsius).

Mountain Climate: The mountainous regions of Southern California experience a more pronounced seasonal variation. Summers are generally cooler and milder compared to the coastal areas, with temperatures averaging in the 70s Fahrenheit (20-26 degrees Celsius). Winters, on the other hand, bring colder temperatures, occasional snowfall, and ski resorts bustling with winter sports enthusiasts.

Desert Climate: The desert regions of Southern California, such as the Mojave Desert, have a desert climate characterized by hot, dry summers and cooler winters. Summer temperatures can soar well above 100 degrees Fahrenheit (38 degrees Celsius), while winter temperatures average around 60-70 degrees Fahrenheit (15-21 degrees Celsius) during the day and can drop significantly at night. These arid regions receive very little rainfall, and the precipitation they do receive often comes in the form of brief but intense thunderstorms during the summer monsoon season.

Inland Valley Climate: The inland valleys of Southern California have a semi-arid climate, with hot, dry summers and cooler, mild winters. Summers can be scorching, with temperatures frequently exceeding 90 degrees Fahrenheit (32 degrees Celsius), while winters are relatively mild, with temperatures ranging from the 60s to low 70s Fahrenheit (15-22 degrees Celsius). These areas receive more rainfall compared to the desert regions, but the overall precipitation is still relatively low.

Climate Challenges

Southern California faces several climate challenges, including droughts, wildfires, and the potential impact of climate change. The region has a history of periodic droughts, which have a significant impact on water resources and agriculture. Water scarcity has led to the implementation of conservation measures, such as water restrictions and the development of innovative water management strategies.

Wildfires are a recurring threat in Southern California, particularly during the dry, windy conditions of late summer and fall. The combination of dry vegetation, strong winds, and high temperatures can fuel these wildfires, posing risks to communities, ecosystems, and air quality.

Climate change is expected to bring further challenges to Southern California. Rising temperatures, changes in rainfall patterns, and the potential for sea-level rise pose risks to the region's ecosystems, infrastructure, and communities. Efforts are underway to mitigate and adapt to these changes, including the promotion of renewable energy, conservation initiatives, and the development of resilient infrastructure.

Southern California's climate and geography create a captivating tapestry of diverse landscapes and ecosystems. From the picturesque coastline to the majestic mountains and vast deserts, the region offers a wealth of natural beauty and outdoor experiences. Understanding the distinct climate patterns and geographical features helps us appreciate the region's unique environmental challenges and the need for sustainable practices to preserve and protect this remarkable area for generations to come.

Local Customs and Etiquette

Welcome to the land of endless sunshine, breathtaking beaches, and a vibrant lifestyle. Southern California, with its unique blend of cultures and diverse communities, is a captivating region that boasts its own distinct set of customs and etiquette. Whether you're a visitor or a new resident, understanding and embracing the local customs will help you immerse yourself in the warm and friendly atmosphere of Southern California.

Here, we'll take a deep dive into the captivating world of local customs and etiquette, uncovering the essence of what makes Southern California a truly special place.

Casual Vibes

Southern California is renowned for its laid-back atmosphere and casual lifestyle. People here tend to adopt a relaxed dress code, favoring comfortable and informal attire for most occasions. From sandy beaches to trendy coffee shops, you'll find locals sporting flip-flops, shorts, and t-shirts throughout the year. So, leave your formal wear at home and embrace the casual vibes of Southern California.

Greetings and Friendliness

Southern Californians are known for their warm and friendly nature. When meeting someone new, a simple smile, a firm handshake, and a friendly "hello" are customary. It's common for people to engage in small talk, so don't be surprised if you find yourself striking up conversations with strangers in coffee shops or while waiting in line. Embrace the friendly atmosphere, and don't hesitate to initiate conversations and build connections with the locals.

Embracing Diversity

Southern California is a melting pot of cultures, and its inhabitants celebrate this diversity. Respect and appreciation for different backgrounds and perspectives are essential in this region. Engage in cultural events, festivals, and culinary experiences to gain a deeper understanding of the rich tapestry of traditions and customs present in Southern California. Remember to approach conversations with an open mind and show genuine interest in learning about the diverse communities around you.

Environmental Consciousness

Southern Californians are environmentally conscious and take pride in their surroundings. The region is renowned for its beautiful landscapes, and locals are committed to preserving them. It is customary to dispose of trash responsibly and participate in recycling programs. Additionally, many communities have embraced sustainable practices, such as using reusable bags and reducing water consumption. Embracing this eco-conscious mindset will earn you appreciation and respect from the locals.

Outdoor Activities

Southern California's year-round pleasant climate provides ample opportunities for outdoor activities. Whether it's hiking, biking, surfing, or enjoying a picnic at the beach, locals take full advantage of their natural surroundings. Respect for public spaces is crucial, so remember to clean up after yourself and follow any posted regulations. Embrace an active lifestyle and join the locals in appreciating the region's scenic beauty and abundant recreational options.

Traffic Etiquette

Southern California is known for its bustling cities and traffic congestion. Patience and courtesy on the road are highly valued. Adhering to traffic laws, signaling lane changes, and allowing others to merge are essential. While traffic can be challenging at times, maintaining a calm and respectful demeanor will go a long way in navigating Southern California's busy streets.

Southern California is a vibrant region that celebrates diversity, warmth, and a laid-back lifestyle. By embracing the local customs and etiquette, you can seamlessly integrate into the fabric of this captivating destination. Remember to embrace the casual vibes, extend friendly greetings, appreciate the diverse communities, practice environmental consciousness, enjoy the great outdoors, and navigate the traffic with patience and courtesy. Whether you're basking in the sun on the beach or exploring the bustling streets of Los Angeles, Southern California welcomes you with open arms and a wealth of enriching experiences.

Best Time To Visit Southern California

Southern California, a sun-kissed utopia nestled along the golden coast of the Pacific Ocean, boasts a year-round allure that captivates travelers from around the world. From the bustling streets of Los Angeles to the serene beaches of San Diego, this region offers an abundance of natural beauty, vibrant cities, and a delightful Mediterranean climate. While Southern California is a haven for tourists throughout the year, there are certain times when the magic truly comes alive. So, let's delve into the best time to visit this captivating destination and unlock the secrets behind each season's unique charm.

Summer (June to August)

Summer in Southern California is synonymous with endless sunshine, warm temperatures, and an electric energy that permeates the air. It's the perfect time for beachgoers and outdoor enthusiasts to indulge in the region's pristine coastline. From the world-famous beaches of Malibu and Santa Monica to the scenic shores of Laguna Beach, you can bask in the sun, surf the waves, and savor the vibrant beach culture. Summer also offers a plethora of outdoor events, including music festivals, county fairs, and outdoor movie screenings, making it an ideal time for a lively and memorable vacation.

Fall (September to November)

As summer transitions into fall, Southern California unveils a new dimension of beauty. The scorching heat mellows, offering pleasantly warm days and cooler nights. Autumn showcases the region's natural wonders, such as the stunning fall foliage in places like Big Bear Lake and Julian, where trees transform into vibrant hues of red, orange, and gold. Fall also marks the start of the harvest season, and visitors can relish the flavors of California's renowned wineries and indulge in seasonal produce at local farmers' markets. With fewer crowds and discounted rates, this is an opportune time to explore popular attractions like Disneyland, Universal Studios, and the Getty Center.

Winter (December to February)

While Southern California may not be the first place that comes to mind for a winter getaway, this season has its own undeniable charm. With average temperatures hovering around 68°F (20°C), winter offers a mild respite from the freezing temperatures found in other parts of the world. You can stroll along the iconic Hollywood Walk of Fame, admire the dazzling holiday lights at the Griffith Observatory, or explore the cultural offerings of the Museum of Contemporary Art in downtown Los Angeles.

Moreover, winter is the prime whale-watching season in Southern California, as majestic gray whales migrate along the coast, creating a truly awe-inspiring spectacle.

Spring (March to May)

Springtime in Southern California is a veritable feast for the senses. The hills come alive with vibrant wildflowers, and the citrus groves emit a fragrant perfume that permeates the air. The temperature begins to warm up, providing ideal conditions for outdoor activities like hiking, biking, and exploring the region's numerous national parks, including Joshua Tree and Channel Islands. Spring is also the season for major events like the Coachella Valley Music and Arts Festival, attracting music enthusiasts from around the globe. The smaller crowds and blooming landscapes make it an excellent time to explore popular attractions like the San Diego Zoo and Balboa Park.

Southern California's enchantment knows no bounds, and each season presents a unique tapestry of experiences for travelers to relish. Whether you seek sunny beaches, cultural immersion, natural beauty, or exciting festivals, there is never a wrong time to visit this captivating destination. From the vibrant energy of summer to the serene allure of spring, Southern California is a paradise that embraces visitors year-round, offering unforgettable memories and a taste of the good life on the Pacific coast. So, pack your bags, embark on an adventure,

Chapter 2: Planning Your Trip To Southern California

Currency and Money Matters

As you embark on your adventure, it's essential to familiarize yourself with currency and money matters to ensure a smooth and hassle-free experience. This guide aims to provide you with valuable information on currency exchange, payment methods, and money-saving tips, allowing you to make the most of your time in this captivating region.

Currency Exchange

The official currency of the United States is the US Dollar ($). South California readily accepts cash, credit cards, and mobile payments, making it convenient for visitors from all corners of the globe. Currency exchange services can be found at airports, banks, and specialized exchange offices throughout the region. While airport exchange rates may not be the most favorable, they do offer convenience. For better rates, consider exchanging your currency at banks or dedicated currency exchange offices found in popular tourist areas.

Credit and Debit Cards

Credit and debit cards are widely accepted in South California, making them a convenient payment method. Visa and Mastercard are widely recognized, with American Express and Discover also accepted at many establishments. It's always a good idea to inform your bank of your travel plans to avoid any potential issues with card usage. Additionally, it's worth checking if your card charges foreign transaction fees, as this can impact your overall expenses.

ATMs

ATMs are abundant throughout South California, allowing you to withdraw cash conveniently. Look for ATMs affiliated with major banks to ensure security and avoid excessive fees. Keep in mind that some ATMs may charge additional fees for international withdrawals, so it's advisable to withdraw larger amounts to minimize transaction charges.

Mobile Payments

The rise of mobile payment platforms has transformed the way people make transactions. In South California, popular options include Apple Pay, Google Pay, and Samsung Pay. These platforms enable you to make secure payments using your smartphone, reducing the need for carrying cash or cards. Many restaurants, shops, and businesses have embraced this technology, so be sure to check if your preferred mobile payment option is accepted.

Tips for Saving Money

Research Dining Options: South California offers a diverse culinary scene, ranging from casual eateries to high-end restaurants. To save money on dining, explore local food trucks, affordable cafes, and explore neighborhood eateries for delicious meals at reasonable prices.

Public Transportation: Utilize public transportation systems, such as buses, trains, and trams, to explore South California. This not only helps reduce transportation costs but also allows you to immerse yourself in the local culture and avoid parking challenges in popular tourist spots.

Discounts and Coupons: Keep an eye out for discounts, coupons, and special offers available at various attractions, museums, and entertainment venues. Local tourism websites, visitor centers, and coupon books often provide valuable savings opportunities.

Free Attractions: South California boasts an array of breathtaking natural wonders and picturesque landscapes that won't cost you a dime. Explore stunning beaches, scenic hiking trails, and captivating parks, allowing you to experience the region's beauty without breaking the bank.

Water and Snacks: Stay hydrated by carrying a reusable water bottle and filling it up at water fountains found in parks and public spaces. Additionally, pack some snacks for your day trips to avoid impulse purchases and save money.

As you embark on your South California adventure, understanding currency and money matters will empower you to make informed decisions and optimize your travel experience. Whether it's exchanging currency, utilizing cards or mobile payments, or employing money-saving tips, being well-prepared ensures a stress-free journey. Embrace the vibrant culture, breathtaking landscapes, and diverse experiences South California has to offer, all while managing your finances effectively.

Visa and Entry Requirements

If you're planning a visit to this sun-soaked region, it's essential to understand the visa and entry requirements to ensure a smooth and hassle-free journey. In this comprehensive guide, we'll explore the visa options available for international visitors, highlight important entry requirements, and provide valuable insights to help you plan your trip to South California.

Visa Waiver Program (VWP)

For citizens of 39 countries, including the United Kingdom, Germany, Australia, Japan, and South Korea, South California's Visa Waiver Program (VWP) offers a convenient way to visit without obtaining a visa. Travelers eligible for the VWP can stay for up to 90 days for tourism or business purposes. It's important to note that travelers must have a valid Electronic System for Travel Authorization (ESTA) approval before boarding a flight to the United States. The ESTA application can be completed online, and a small fee is charged.

Visitor Visas

If you're not eligible for the VWP or planning an extended stay in South California, you'll need to apply for a visitor visa. The B-2 tourist visa is commonly used for tourism, vacations, medical treatment, or participation in social events. To obtain a visitor visa, you must schedule an interview at the nearest U.S. embassy or consulate in your home country. During the interview, you'll need to demonstrate the purpose of your trip, strong ties to your home country, and the intention to return after your visit.

Passport Requirements

A valid passport is an essential document for entry into South California. Your passport must be valid for at least six months beyond your intended stay in the United States. It's recommended to review your passport's validity well in advance and renew it if necessary, as airlines and immigration officials strictly enforce this requirement.

Customs and Border Protection (CBP) Process

Upon arrival in South California, you'll go through the Customs and Border Protection (CBP) process. Be prepared to present your passport, completed customs declaration form, and any supporting documents related to your trip. CBP officers may ask about the purpose of your visit, your accommodation details, and the duration of your stay, so it's advisable to have these details readily available.

Entry Fees

As of the time of writing, South California does not impose any entry fees or charges for visitors entering the region. However, it's essential to stay informed about any changes in visa fees or entry requirements by visiting the official websites of the U.S. Department of State and the U.S. Customs and Border Protection.

COVID-19 Travel Considerations

Given the global pandemic, it's crucial to stay updated on any travel restrictions or guidelines related to COVID-19. Before your trip, check the official websites of the U.S. Department of State, the Centers for Disease Control and Prevention (CDC), and the local health authorities in South California for the latest information on entry requirements, testing protocols, and quarantine regulations.

South California beckons with its irresistible blend of diverse cultures, breathtaking landscapes, and exciting attractions. By understanding the visa and entry requirements outlined in this guide, you can ensure a seamless travel experience to this enchanting region. Whether you're planning a short getaway or an extended adventure, be sure to stay informed, complete the necessary paperwork, and comply with all regulations, allowing you to focus on creating unforgettable memories in South California.

Health and Safety Tips

While you embark on your exciting journey, it's essential to prioritize your health and safety. This comprehensive guide will provide you with valuable tips to ensure a safe and enjoyable visit to Southern California.

Protect Yourself from the Sun

With its sunny climate, Southern California offers endless opportunities for outdoor activities. However, prolonged sun exposure can lead to sunburns and heat-related illnesses. Follow these tips to stay safe:

- Wear sunscreen with a high SPF, preferably above 30, and reapply it every two hours.
- Utilize wide-brimmed hats, sunglasses, and lightweight, breathable clothing to protect your skin.

- Seek shade during the hottest hours of the day, typically between 10 am and 4 pm.
- Stay hydrated by drinking plenty of water and avoid excessive alcohol or caffeine intake.

Stay Hydrated

The warm climate in Southern California can be dehydrating, especially if you engage in physical activities or spend extended periods outdoors. Stay hydrated by following these guidelines:

- Carry a refillable water bottle and drink water regularly, even if you don't feel thirsty.
- Avoid excessive consumption of sugary drinks and alcohol, as they can contribute to dehydration.
- Opt for hydrating foods such as fruits and vegetables, which have high water content.

Practice Water Safety

Southern California boasts breathtaking beaches and inviting waters, but it's crucial to prioritize water safety:

- Swim only in designated areas with lifeguards present and adhere to their instructions.
- Pay attention to warning signs, flags, and currents. Riptides can be dangerous, so if caught in one, swim parallel to the shore until you're free from its pull.
- Keep a close eye on children and inexperienced swimmers at all times.
- Familiarize yourself with basic water rescue techniques and learn CPR.

Be Mindful of Wildlife

Southern California is home to diverse wildlife, including marine animals, insects, and reptiles. To coexist harmoniously, keep these tips in mind:

- Do not approach or feed wild animals, as it disrupts their natural behavior and can be dangerous.

- Be cautious of stinging insects such as bees and wasps. If you encounter them, remain calm and slowly move away.
- If hiking or exploring nature reserves, stay on designated trails to minimize your impact on the ecosystem and reduce the risk of encounters with venomous snakes.

Maintain Road Safety

If you plan to explore Southern California by car, prioritize road safety:

- Familiarize yourself with local traffic laws and regulations.
- Always wear your seatbelt and ensure all passengers do the same.
- Avoid using handheld devices while driving. If you need to use your phone, pull over to a safe location.
- Plan your routes in advance, allowing extra time for traffic, and be mindful of rush hour periods.

Follow COVID-19 Guidelines

Given the ongoing COVID-19 pandemic, it's crucial to prioritize public health and follow the guidelines set forth by health authorities:

- Wear masks in indoor public spaces and outdoor areas where social distancing is not possible.
- Practice frequent hand hygiene by washing your hands with soap and water for at least 20 seconds or using hand sanitizer when soap is unavailable.
- Maintain social distancing of at least six feet from individuals outside your travel group.
- Stay informed about local guidelines and any travel restrictions that may be in place.

Be Prepared for Earthquakes

Southern California is situated in an area prone to earthquakes. While they are relatively rare, it's essential to be prepared and know what to do in case of an earthquake:

- Familiarize yourself with earthquake safety procedures, such as "Drop, Cover, and Hold On." When an earthquake strikes, drop to the ground, take cover under a sturdy piece of furniture, and hold on until the shaking stops.
- If you are outdoors during an earthquake, move away from buildings, streetlights, and utility wires to avoid potential hazards.
- Stay informed about local emergency services and have a basic emergency kit ready, including essential supplies like water, non-perishable food, flashlights, batteries, and a first aid kit.

Stay Vigilant in Crowded Areas

Southern California's popular attractions and bustling cities can be crowded, especially during peak tourist seasons. Here are some tips for staying safe in crowded areas:

- Keep your belongings secure by using a cross-body bag or keeping valuables in a front pocket.
- Be cautious of pickpockets and stay vigilant in crowded places, such as public transportation, markets, and busy tourist spots.
- Avoid displaying large sums of money or valuable jewelry openly to minimize the risk of theft.
- Trust your instincts. If a situation feels unsafe or uncomfortable, remove yourself from it and seek assistance if necessary.

Respect Local Customs and Regulations

When visiting Southern California, it's essential to respect local customs, traditions, and regulations:

- Observe and follow any signage or instructions provided by authorities at tourist sites, parks, and public spaces.
- Be mindful of noise levels, especially in residential areas, and avoid disturbing the

peace and tranquility of local communities.

- Familiarize yourself with local laws, including smoking regulations, alcohol consumption rules, and restrictions on recreational activities.

Seek Medical Assistance if needed

In the event of a medical emergency or if you require medical assistance during your trip, remember the following:

- Save the contact information of emergency services, local hospitals, and healthcare facilities in your phone or keep them readily available.
- Purchase travel insurance that covers medical expenses and offers assistance in case of emergencies.
- If you require prescription medication, ensure you have an adequate supply for the duration of your trip, and carry them in their original labeled containers.

By adhering to these health and safety tips, you can fully enjoy your visit to Southern California while minimizing potential risks. Remember, being proactive about your well-being allows you to make the most of your experience and create lasting memories in this beautiful region.

What To Pack

Whether you're planning a trip to Los Angeles, San Diego, or any other stunning destination in the region, packing strategically will ensure you make the most of your visit. In this comprehensive guide, we'll explore the essential items you should pack to have a memorable and comfortable experience in Southern California.

Sun Protection Essentials

Southern California is renowned for its sunny climate. To shield yourself from the strong rays, don't forget to pack the following:

- **Sunscreen with a high SPF:** Protect your skin from harmful UV rays by using a broad-spectrum sunscreen with an SPF of 30 or higher.
- **Sunglasses**: Invest in a good pair of sunglasses to protect your eyes from the intense sunlight.
- **Wide-brimmed hat:** A stylish hat will not only elevate your outfit but also provide additional shade and protect your face from the sun.

Light and Breathable Clothing

Southern California enjoys a Mediterranean climate with mild winters and warm to hot summers. Pack the following clothing items to stay comfortable throughout your trip:

- **T-shirts and tank tops:** Opt for lightweight and breathable fabrics to stay cool during the day.
- **Shorts and skirts:** Pack a few pairs of shorts and skirts to pair with your tops.

They are perfect for beach outings and exploring the coastal areas.

- **Lightweight pants and long-sleeved shirts:** These items will come in handy during cooler evenings or if you plan to visit higher elevations.
- **Swimsuits:** Don't forget to pack your swimsuit for a refreshing dip in the Pacific Ocean or for relaxing by the pool.

Comfortable Footwear

Exploring Southern California often involves walking, so pack comfortable shoes to keep your feet happy:

- Walking shoes or sneakers: Opt for well-fitting, supportive shoes suitable for hiking, sightseeing, and exploring urban areas.
- Sandals or flip-flops: Perfect for the beach, strolling along the boardwalk, or simply relaxing.

Layering Options

Southern California's weather can be variable, especially in coastal regions. Pack these items to be prepared for temperature fluctuations:

- Lightweight jacket or sweater: Evenings can be cooler, so a light layer will keep you comfortable during nighttime outings.
- Scarf or shawl: A versatile accessory that can be used as a fashion statement or to keep warm during chilly evenings.

Beach and Outdoor Essentials

Make the most of Southern California's stunning coastline and natural beauty with these beach and outdoor essentials:

- **Beach towel or mat**: Ideal for lounging on the beach or picnicking in the parks.
- **Beach bag:** A spacious bag to carry your essentials like sunscreen, sunglasses, a book, and snacks.
- **Hiking gear:** If you plan to explore Southern California's numerous hiking trails, pack appropriate gear such as sturdy

shoes, a backpack, a water bottle, and a hat.

Electronics and Miscellaneous Items

Ensure you have the necessary gadgets and accessories to capture memories and stay connected:

- Camera or smartphone: Southern California offers countless picturesque moments, so don't forget your camera or smartphone with a good camera.
- Power bank: Keep your devices charged while you're out and about.
- Universal power adapter: If you're traveling from outside the United States, this will come in handy for charging your electronics.

Packing smartly for your trip to Southern California will enhance your experience and ensure you're prepared for its diverse offerings. From sunscreen and comfortable footwear to versatile clothing options and beach essentials, this comprehensive guide covers the must-pack items for a memorable visit to the enchanting Southern California. By prioritizing sun protection, lightweight and breathable clothing, comfortable footwear, layering options, beach and outdoor essentials, as well as necessary electronics and miscellaneous items, you'll be well-prepared for everything this captivating region has to offer.

With the right essentials in your suitcase, you'll be ready to soak up the sunshine on the stunning beaches, explore vibrant cities, embark on breathtaking hikes, and immerse yourself in the rich cultural tapestry of Southern California. So pack wisely, embrace the spirit of adventure, and get ready to create unforgettable memories in this enchanting part of the world.

Transportation Options

Southern California is a vast and diverse region with a lot to offer visitors. From the bustling city of Los Angeles to the laid-back beach town of San Diego, there's something for everyone in SoCal. And with so much to see and do, it's important to have a good transportation plan in place.

Here are a few of the transportation options available in Southern California:

Public transportation: Southern California has a well-developed public transportation system, making it easy to get around without a car. The Los Angeles County Metropolitan Transportation Authority (Metro) operates a network of buses, trains, and light rail lines that serve the greater Los Angeles area. Metrolink is a commuter rail service that connects Los Angeles with cities in the surrounding area, including Orange, Riverside, and San Bernardino Counties. The San Diego Metropolitan Transit System (MTS) operates a network of buses, trains, and trolleys that serve the greater San Diego area.

Car rental: If you're planning on doing a lot of exploring, renting a car is a great option. This will give you the freedom to go where you want, when you want. There are a number of car rental companies to choose from, so you can find the best deal for your needs.

Ride-hailing services: Ride-hailing services like Uber and Lyft are a convenient and affordable way to get around. You can request a ride from your phone, and the driver will pick you up at your location. Ride-hailing services are available in most major cities in Southern California.

Taxis: Taxis are another option for getting around Southern California. They are available in most major cities, and you can hail them on the street or call for one. Taxis can be more expensive than other forms of transportation, but they are a reliable option.

Biking: Biking is a great way to get around Southern California, especially in the warmer months. There are a number of bike lanes and trails throughout the region, making it easy to get around without a car. Biking can be a great way to see the sights and get some exercise at the same time.

Walking: Walking is another great way to get around Southern California, especially in the city centers. Many of the major cities in SoCal have walkable downtown areas with shops, restaurants, and attractions within easy walking distance. Walking is a great way to get some fresh air and exercise, and it can also save you money on transportation costs. No matter how you choose to get around, Southern California is a great place to explore.

Driving in Southern California

Whether you're interested in exploring the bustling cities of Los Angeles and San Diego, the stunning beaches of Malibu and Newport, or the rugged mountains of Big Bear and Joshua Tree, you're sure to find something to love in Southern California.

One of the best ways to experience all that Southern California has to offer is by car. With its well-maintained roads and scenic routes, driving in Southern California is a pleasure. However, there are a few things that visitors should keep in mind before hitting the road.

1. Be prepared for traffic - Southern California is a major metropolitan area, and traffic can be heavy, especially during rush hour. If you're planning on driving during peak times, be sure to allow plenty of extra time for your trip.

2. Be aware of the speed limit - The speed limit on freeways in Southern California is 65 mph. If you're caught speeding, you'll be hit with a hefty fine.

3. Use your turn signals - This may seem like a no-brainer, but it's important to use your turn signals in Southern California, even if you think it's obvious where you're going. Many drivers in Southern California are aggressive and impatient, so it's important to be clear about your intentions.

4. Be aware of the weather - The weather in Southern California can change quickly, so it's important to be prepared for anything. If you're driving in the mountains, be sure to pack a jacket or sweater, even if it's warm in the valley. And if you're driving during the summer, be sure to pack plenty of water and sunscreen.

5. Enjoy the drive - Southern California is a beautiful place, and there's no better way to see it than by car. So relax, put on some good music, and enjoy the ride.

Here are some additional tips for driving in Southern California:

* If you're renting a car, be sure to ask about the insurance policy. Many rental car companies have a "collision damage waiver" (CDW) that can protect you from paying for damage to the car if you're in an accident.

* If you're driving in a city, be sure to familiarize yourself with the local traffic laws. Many cities have different rules for parking, turning, and lane usage.

* If you're driving in a rural area, be sure to watch out for wildlife. Deer, coyotes, and other animals are often seen on the side of the road.

* If you're driving during the summer, be sure to drink plenty of water and stay hydrated. The heat can be very intense in Southern California, especially in the desert.

With a little planning and preparation, driving in Southern California can be a safe and enjoyable experience. So get out there and explore all that this beautiful region has to offer.

Chapter 3: Exploring Los Angeles

Top Attractions in Los Angeles

Los Angeles is one of the most popular tourist destinations in the world, and for good reason. With its sunny weather, stunning beaches, and endless entertainment options, there's something for everyone in LA.

Here are some of the top attractions to visit in Los Angeles:

Hollywood Walk of Fame - The Hollywood Walk of Fame is a must-see for any visitor to Los Angeles. This iconic walkway is lined with stars bearing the names of some of the biggest names in Hollywood history. You can take a self-guided tour or join a guided tour to learn more about the history of the Walk of Fame and the celebrities who are honored there.

Hollywood Sign - The Hollywood Sign is another iconic Los Angeles landmark. This giant sign is perched on Mount Lee and offers stunning views of the city. You can hike to the sign or take a shuttle bus to get up close.

Griffith Observatory - The Griffith Observatory is a great place to learn about astronomy and enjoy stunning views of the city. The observatory is open to the public and offers free admission.

Universal Studios Hollywood - Universal Studios Hollywood is a popular theme park that offers a behind-the-scenes look at the making of movies and TV shows. The park also has thrilling rides and attractions based on popular films and TV shows.

Disneyland Resort - Disneyland Resort is another popular theme park located in Anaheim, California. The resort is home to two theme parks, Disneyland and Disney California Adventure, as well as a shopping, dining, and entertainment district called Downtown Disney District.

Venice Beach Boardwalk - The Venice Beach Boardwalk is a lively beachfront area with a unique atmosphere. The boardwalk is home to street performers, artists, and vendors, as well as a variety of shops and restaurants.

Santa Monica Pier - The Santa Monica Pier is another popular beachfront destination. The pier is home to a variety of rides, games, and attractions, as well as a number of restaurants and shops.

Getty Center - The Getty Center is a world-renowned art museum located in Brentwood, California. The museum houses a collection of over 160,000 works of art, including paintings, sculptures, and photographs.

Los Angeles County Museum of Art (LACMA) - LACMA is one of the largest and most comprehensive art museums in the United States. The museum houses a collection of over 120,000 works of art, including paintings, sculptures, and photographs.

The Broad - The Broad is a contemporary art museum located in Downtown Los Angeles. The museum houses a collection of over 2,000 works of art, including paintings, sculptures, and installations.

These are just a few of the many top attractions to visit in Los Angeles. With so much to see and do, you're sure to have a memorable trip to this vibrant city.

Best Neighborhoods To Explore

Los Angeles is a sprawling metropolis with something for everyone. From the iconic Hollywood sign to the beautiful beaches of Santa Monica, there's no shortage of things to see and do in this vibrant city. But with so many neighborhoods to choose from, it can be hard to know where to start.

Here are a few of the best neighborhoods to explore in Los Angeles:

Hollywood - is one of the most famous neighborhoods in the world, and for good reason. This is where you'll find the Walk of Fame, the Chinese Theatre, and the Dolby Theatre, home to the Academy Awards. Hollywood is also home to a vibrant nightlife scene, with bars, clubs, and restaurants to suit every taste.

Beverly Hills - is another iconic Los Angeles neighborhood. This upscale area is home to some of the most expensive real estate in the world, as well as designer boutiques, fine dining restaurants, and luxury hotels. Beverly Hills is also home to the Beverly Hills Hotel, the Playboy Mansion, and Rodeo Drive.

Santa Monica - is a popular beachside destination with a laid-back atmosphere. This neighborhood is home to the Santa Monica Pier, Third Street Promenade, and Santa Monica Beach. Santa Monica is also home to a variety of art galleries, museums, and theaters.

Venice Beach - is a unique and eclectic neighborhood with a bohemian vibe. This neighborhood is home to the Venice Beach Boardwalk, Muscle Beach, and Venice Beach Canals. Venice Beach is also home to a variety of art galleries, shops, and restaurants.

Los Feliz - is a charming neighborhood with a mix of old and new. This neighborhood is home to Griffith Park, the Hollywood Bowl, and the Los Feliz Village. Los Feliz is also home to a variety of coffee shops, restaurants, and bars.

These are just a few of the many great neighborhoods to explore in Los Angeles. With so much to see and do, you're sure to find something to your liking in this vibrant city.

Here are some additional tips for exploring Los Angeles neighborhoods:

Take your time: Don't try to see too much in one day. Take your time and explore each neighborhood at your own pace.

Get off the beaten path: Don't just stick to the tourist areas. Venture out into the less-known neighborhoods and you'll be rewarded with a more authentic experience.

Talk to the locals: The best way to learn about a neighborhood is to talk to the people who live there. Ask them for recommendations on places to eat, drink, and see.

Be open to new experiences: Los Angeles is a city of diversity. Be open to new experiences and you'll be sure to have a memorable trip.

Beaches and Coastal Areas

When it comes to the perfect blend of sun, sand, and surf, Los Angeles stands out as a coastal paradise. Renowned for its iconic beaches and breathtaking coastal areas, the city offers a diverse range of experiences for beach enthusiasts, adventure seekers, and nature lovers alike. Here, we will delve into some of the most captivating beaches and coastal areas in Los Angeles that are worth exploring. Get ready to dive into a world of natural beauty, vibrant communities, and endless coastal adventures.

Santa Monica Beach and Pier

Let's start with one of the most iconic and beloved beach destinations in Los Angeles: Santa Monica Beach. Stretching three and a half miles along the picturesque coastline, this beach boasts golden sands, beautiful views of the Pacific Ocean, and a vibrant atmosphere. Take a stroll along the world-famous Santa Monica Pier, where you can enjoy thrilling rides, indulge in delicious seafood, and witness breathtaking sunsets. Don't miss the chance to visit the bustling Third Street Promenade, known for its trendy shops, street performers, and delectable dining options.

Venice Beach and Boardwalk

Just a stone's throw away from Santa Monica, you'll find another coastal gem—Venice Beach. Known for its vibrant and eclectic atmosphere, this beach captures the essence of the bohemian spirit. Take a walk along the colorful Venice Boardwalk, where you'll encounter street performers, local artists, and quirky vendors. Indulge in some people-watching as you witness the unique blend of cultures, skateboarding enthusiasts, and bodybuilders at the famous Muscle Beach. You can also explore the Venice Canals, a charming residential area inspired by the Italian city.

Malibu

A short drive up the Pacific Coast Highway will lead you to the enchanting coastal community of Malibu. Nestled between the Santa Monica Mountains and the Pacific Ocean, Malibu offers a blend of natural beauty and celebrity allure. With its pristine beaches, including Zuma Beach and El Matador State Beach, you can relax on the sandy shores or catch some waves. Don't miss the opportunity to explore Malibu Creek State Park, offering hiking trails, stunning vistas, and the iconic Rock Pool.

Leo Carrillo State Park

For those seeking a more secluded and pristine coastal experience, Leo Carrillo State Park is an ideal choice. Located north of Malibu, this hidden gem offers tide pools, sea caves, and coastal cliffs that provide a picturesque backdrop for nature enthusiasts. Explore the trails that wind through the park, enjoy a picnic by the beach, or try your hand at surfing and swimming in the refreshing waters. Camping facilities are also available for those who wish to extend their stay and immerse themselves in the tranquility of the park.

Point Dume State Beach

Situated at the western end of Malibu, Point Dume State Beach is a captivating destination that rewards visitors with stunning coastal vistas and diverse marine life. Climb up the rocky promontory and be rewarded with breathtaking panoramic views of the coastline and the Santa Monica Bay. This beach is a haven for wildlife enthusiasts, offering the opportunity to spot seals, dolphins, and even migrating gray whales during the winter months. Explore the hidden coves, walk along the sandy shores, or venture into the crystal-clear waters for a snorkeling adventure.

Los Angeles is not just a city of glitz and glamour; it also boasts an incredible coastline that offers a wide range of experiences for beach lovers. Whether you're seeking a bustling and lively atmosphere or a secluded coastal escape, the beaches and coastal areas of Los Angeles have it all. From the iconic Santa Monica Beach to the vibrant Venice Boardwalk, and the scenic beauty of Malibu and the hidden gems like Leo Carrillo State Park and Point Dume State Beach, there's something for everyone.

These beaches and coastal areas not only provide opportunities for sunbathing and swimming but also offer a host of activities for outdoor enthusiasts. Surfing, paddleboarding, kayaking, and beach volleyball are just a few of the popular water sports you can enjoy. The consistent waves and favorable weather conditions make these beaches a surfer's paradise, attracting wave riders from all skill levels.

Nature lovers will find solace in the pristine beauty and diverse ecosystems found along the Los Angeles coastline. The tide pools at Leo Carrillo State Park and Point Dume State Beach are teeming with fascinating marine life, providing an excellent opportunity for exploration and discovery. Keep an eye out for starfish, anemones, hermit crabs, and various colorful fish.

For hikers and nature enthusiasts, the coastal trails in these areas offer breathtaking views of the ocean and the surrounding landscapes. Take a leisurely stroll along the beach, venture into the rugged cliffs, or explore the lush coastal canyons. The trails in Malibu Creek State Park, for instance, lead to hidden waterfalls and offer a chance to immerse yourself in the serenity of nature.

Photography enthusiasts will be delighted by the picturesque settings these beaches provide. Capture stunning sunsets over the Pacific Ocean, unique rock formations, and the vibrant atmosphere of the boardwalks. These locations offer endless opportunities to create memorable and Instagram-worthy shots.

Apart from the natural beauty, the coastal areas of Los Angeles are home to vibrant communities with a rich cultural heritage. The beachfront neighborhoods of Santa Monica and Venice Beach are renowned for their artsy vibe, bustling markets, street performers, and lively nightlife. Explore the local shops, dine at beachside cafes, and immerse yourself in the unique blend of cultures that make these areas so special.

The beaches and coastal areas of Los Angeles offer a diverse range of experiences that cater to all interests. From the iconic Santa Monica Beach and Venice Boardwalk to the tranquil beauty of Malibu and the hidden gems like Leo Carrillo State Park and Point Dume State Beach, there's an abundance of natural beauty, outdoor activities, and vibrant communities to explore. Whether you're seeking relaxation, adventure, or a cultural experience, Los Angeles has it all on its captivating coastline. So grab your sunscreen, towel, and sense of adventure, and embark on an unforgettable coastal journey in the City of Angels.

Where To Eat and Drink

Los Angeles is a city of diversity, and that diversity is reflected in its food scene. From world-class sushi to authentic Mexican cuisine, there's something for everyone in LA. Here are a few of the best places to eat and drink in the city:

Maude - This Michelin-starred restaurant offers a tasting menu of modern American cuisine. The dishes are beautifully presented and the service is impeccable.

The Bazaar by José Andrés: This Spanish tapas restaurant is a must-visit for anyone who loves food. The menu changes daily, but you can always expect creative and delicious dishes.

Providence: This seafood restaurant is located in the heart of Beverly Hills. The menu features fresh, locally-sourced seafood, and the wine list is extensive.

The Tasting Kitchen: This Santa Monica restaurant offers a tasting menu of California cuisine. The dishes are seasonal and the wine list is well-curated.

The Grill on the Alley: This Beverly Hills institution is a great place to go for a power lunch or a special occasion dinner. The menu features classic American dishes, and the wine list is extensive.

If you're looking for something more casual, here are a few great options:

Guisados: This Mexican chain is known for its delicious tacos. The tacos are made with fresh, high-quality ingredients and the prices are very reasonable.

Howlin' Ray's: This Nashville hot chicken joint is a must-try for anyone who loves spicy food. The chicken is fried to perfection and the heat level is adjustable, so you can find the perfect level of spice for your taste.

Grand Central Market: This historic market is home to a variety of food vendors, so you can find something to your taste no matter what you're in the mood for.

The Original Farmers Market: This iconic market is a great place to find fresh produce, flowers, and prepared foods. There are also a variety of restaurants and cafes, so you can grab a bite to eat while you're shopping.

The Venice Beach Boardwalk: This iconic boardwalk is lined with food vendors, so you can find everything from hot dogs and pizza to ice cream and churros. There are also a variety of restaurants and bars, so you can find a place to relax and enjoy the views.

No matter what your budget or taste, you're sure to find something to your liking in Los Angeles. So next time you're in the city, be sure to check out some of these great places to eat and drink.

Here are some additional tips for finding the best places to eat and drink in Los Angeles:

* Ask your friends and family for recommendations. They'll know your taste and can point you in the right direction.

* Read online reviews. This is a great way to get an idea of what other people think of a particular restaurant or bar.

* Check out social media. Many restaurants and bars have active social media accounts where they post about their menus, specials, and events.

* Visit the restaurant or bar in person. This is the best way to see if it's a good fit for you.

With a little planning, you're sure to have a delicious and memorable dining experience in Los Angeles.

Accommodations in Los Angeles

Los Angeles is a sprawling metropolis with something to offer everyone. From world-famous attractions like Hollywood and the Walk of Fame to stunning beaches and hiking trails, there's no shortage of things to see and do in LA. But with so much to see and do, it can be tough to find a place to stay that's both affordable and convenient.

That's where this list comes in. Here are 10 nice and affordable accommodation options to stay in as a tourist visiting Los Angeles:

Freehand Los Angeles

Freehand Los Angeles is a stylish hostel located in the heart of Downtown LA. The hostel offers a variety of room types, including private rooms, dormitories, and even a rooftop pool. Freehand Los Angeles is also home to a number of on-site amenities, including a restaurant, bar, and coffee shop. Prices start at $79 per night.

BLVD Hotel & Suites

BLVD Hotel & Suites is a modern hotel located in the Koreatown neighborhood of Los Angeles. The hotel offers a variety of room types, including standard rooms, suites, and even a penthouse. BLVD Hotel & Suites is also home to a number of on-site amenities, including a restaurant, bar, and fitness center. Prices start at $109 per night.

Hotel Angeleno

Hotel Angeleno is a boutique hotel located in the Echo Park neighborhood of Los Angeles. The hotel offers a variety of room types, including standard rooms, suites, and even a rooftop pool.

Hotel Angeleno is also home to a number of on-site amenities, including a restaurant, bar, and fitness center. Prices start at $129 per night.

Hotel June

Hotel June is a historic hotel located in the West Hollywood neighborhood of Los Angeles. The hotel offers a variety of room types, including standard rooms, suites, and even a penthouse. Hotel June is also home to a number of on-site amenities, including a restaurant, bar, and fitness center. Prices start at $149 per night.

Mama Shelter

Mama Shelter is a trendy hotel located in the Arts District of Los Angeles. The hotel offers a variety of room types, including standard rooms, suites, and even a rooftop pool. Mama Shelter is also home to a number of on-site amenities, including a restaurant, bar, and fitness center. Prices start at $169 per night.

The Hoxton, Williamsburg

The Hoxton, Williamsburg is a stylish hotel located in the Fairfax District of Los Angeles. The hotel offers a variety of room types, including standard rooms, suites, and even a rooftop pool. The Hoxton, Williamsburg is also home to a number of on-site amenities, including a restaurant, bar, and fitness center. Prices start at $189 per night.

The Standard, Downtown LA

The Standard, Downtown LA is a hip hotel located in the Financial District of Los Angeles. The hotel offers a variety of room types, including standard rooms, suites, and even a rooftop pool. The Standard, Downtown LA is also home to a number of on-site amenities, including a restaurant, bar, and fitness center. Prices start at $209 per night.

The Westin Bonaventure Hotel & Suites

The Westin Bonaventure Hotel & Suites is a luxury hotel located in the Downtown LA Bunker Hill neighborhood. The hotel offers a variety of room types, including standard rooms, suites, and even a rooftop pool. The Westin Bonaventure Hotel & Suites is also home to a number of on-site amenities, including a restaurant, bar, and fitness center. Prices start at $229 per night.

The Ritz-Carlton, Marina del Rey

The Ritz-Carlton, Marina del Rey is a five-star hotel located in the Marina del Rey neighborhood of Los Angeles. The hotel offers a variety of room types, including standard rooms, suites, and even a rooftop pool. The Ritz-Carlton, Marina del Rey is also home to a number of on-site amenities, including a restaurant, bar, and fitness center. Prices start at $249 per night.

The Beverly Hills Hotel

The Beverly Hills Hotel is an iconic hotel located in the Beverly Hills neighborhood of Los Angeles. The hotel offers a variety of room types, including standard rooms, suites, and even a pool. The Beverly Hills Hotel is also home to a number of on-site amenities, including a restaurant, bar, and fitness center. Prices start at $269 per night.

Shopping and Fashion

Los Angeles is a city of dreams, and for many people, that dream includes shopping. With its diverse population and endless options, LA is a shopper's paradise. From high-end boutiques to thrift stores, there's something for everyone in this city.

If you're looking to splurge, Rodeo Drive is the place to be. This iconic street is home to some of the most exclusive brands in the world, including Gucci, Dior, and Chanel. If you're on a budget, don't worry - there are plenty of other great places to shop in LA. The Grove and The

Americana are two popular outdoor malls with a wide variety of stores. Melrose Avenue is another great option, with its mix of high-end and independent boutiques.

And if you're looking for something unique, don't miss the Santee Alley. This sprawling outdoor market is home to hundreds of vendors selling everything from clothes and accessories to electronics and home goods. You're sure to find a bargain here.

No matter what your budget or style, you're sure to find something to love in LA. So get out there and start shopping!

Here are some specific tips for shopping in LA:

Do your research: Before you go shopping, take some time to research the different areas and stores that you want to visit. This will help you make the most of your time and avoid wasting time on stores that you're not interested in.

Be prepared to walk: Los Angeles is a big city, and you'll likely be doing a lot of walking if you plan on doing a lot of shopping. Make sure to wear comfortable shoes and bring a water bottle.

Don't be afraid to bargain: In many parts of LA, it's customary to bargain with the vendors. This is especially true at the Santee Alley.

Be aware of your surroundings: Los Angeles is a big city, and it's important to be aware of your surroundings when you're out shopping. Keep your valuables close to you and be aware of any suspicious activity.

With these tips in mind, you're sure to have a great time shopping in LA. So get out there and start exploring.

Chapter 4: Discovering San Diego

Top Attractions in San Diego

San Diego is a city with something for everyone. From its world-famous zoo to its beautiful beaches, there's something to keep everyone entertained. Here are some of the top attractions to visit in San Diego:

San Diego Zoo: The San Diego Zoo is one of the most popular tourist attractions in the world. It's home to over 3,500 animals from all over the globe, including pandas, gorillas, and polar bears. The zoo is also known for its innovative exhibits, such as the Polar Bear Plunge and the Elephant Odyssey.

Balboa Park: Balboa Park is a 1,200-acre urban park in the heart of San Diego. It's home to over 15 museums, theaters, gardens, and other attractions. Some of the most popular attractions in Balboa Park include the San Diego Zoo, the San Diego Air & Space Museum, and the Japanese Friendship Garden.

SeaWorld San Diego: SeaWorld San Diego is a marine mammal park that's home to over 3,000 animals, including dolphins, whales, and sea lions. The park offers a variety of shows and exhibits, as well as opportunities to interact with the animals.

USS Midway Museum: The USS Midway Museum is an aircraft carrier that's been converted into a museum. The ship is open to the public and offers tours, exhibits, and educational programs.

La Jolla: La Jolla is a coastal community in San Diego that's known for its beautiful beaches, coves, and tide pools. The area is also home to a number of art galleries, boutiques, and restaurants.

Torrey Pines State Natural Reserve: Torrey Pines State Natural Reserve is a coastal park that's home to a rare type of pine tree. The park offers hiking trails, stunning views of the Pacific Ocean, and opportunities to see wildlife such as coyotes, bobcats, and sea lions.

Petco Park: Petco Park is a baseball stadium that's home to the San Diego Padres. The park is known for its beautiful views of the city skyline and its lively atmosphere.

Gaslamp Quarter: The Gaslamp Quarter is a historic district in downtown San Diego. The area is home to a variety of Victorian-era buildings, shops, restaurants, and bars.

Old Town San Diego State Historic Park: Old Town San Diego State Historic Park is a living history museum that recreates the city's early days. The park is home to a variety of historical buildings, shops, and restaurants.

Cabrillo National Monument: Cabrillo National Monument is a historic site that commemorates the landing of Juan Rodríguez Cabrillo, the first European to set foot on the West Coast of the United States. The monument offers stunning views of the Pacific Ocean and opportunities to learn about the history of the area.

These are just a few of the many top attractions for tourists visiting San Diego. With its beautiful beaches, warm climate, and abundance of activities, San Diego is a city that has something for everyone.

Best Neighborhoods To Explore

San Diego, known as America's Finest City, offers a wealth of breathtaking sights, vibrant culture, and a laid-back coastal lifestyle. While the city boasts famous attractions like the San Diego Zoo, Balboa Park, and the Gaslamp Quarter, its true charm lies in its diverse and unique neighborhoods. From beachfront communities to historic districts, each neighborhood in San Diego has its own distinct character and allure. Let's embark on an unforgettable journey as we uncover the best neighborhoods to explore when visiting this coastal gem.

La Jolla

Located along the rugged coastline, La Jolla is a picturesque neighborhood with dramatic cliffs, stunning ocean views, and pristine beaches. Take a stroll along the iconic La Jolla Cove, where you can spot seals and sea lions basking in the sun. Explore the charming village, home to upscale boutiques, art galleries, and exquisite dining establishments. Don't miss the chance to visit the Birch Aquarium and witness captivating marine life up close.

Little Italy

Immerse yourself in the vibrant ambiance of Little Italy, a trendy neighborhood that pays homage to its Italian roots. This bustling district offers a delightful array of Italian restaurants, sidewalk cafes, and gelato shops. Visit the Mercato—a bustling farmers' market held every Saturday—where you can savor local produce, artisanal goods, and live music. Be sure to check out the art galleries and street murals that contribute to the neighborhood's artistic flair.

North Park

For a hip and eclectic experience, head to North Park, San Diego's cultural hotspot. Known for its thriving craft beer scene, this neighborhood boasts numerous breweries and beer bars where you can sample unique and flavorful brews. Explore the quirky boutiques, vintage shops, and trendy eateries along University Avenue. Visit the iconic Observatory North Park, a historic theater that hosts concerts and events throughout the year.

Coronado

Cross the iconic Coronado Bridge and step into the charming island community of Coronado. This idyllic neighborhood is renowned for its pristine beaches, luxurious resorts, and the iconic Hotel del Coronado—an architectural marvel. Take a leisurely bike ride or stroll along the Coronado Beach, soak in the awe-inspiring views of the Pacific Ocean, and marvel at the historic Victorian homes that line the streets.

Barrio Logan

Immerse yourself in San Diego's rich cultural heritage by exploring the vibrant Barrio Logan neighborhood. This eclectic district is a hub of Chicano art, delicious Mexican cuisine, and community-driven initiatives. Visit Chicano Park, a National Historic Landmark adorned with vibrant murals that celebrate the neighborhood's cultural identity. Explore the art galleries and studios, where you can witness the creativity and talent of local artists firsthand.

Point Loma

Discover the nautical charm of Point Loma, a neighborhood rich in maritime history and breathtaking vistas. Visit Cabrillo National Monument and climb to the top of the Old Point Loma Lighthouse for panoramic views of San Diego Bay and the Pacific Ocean. Explore the tide pools at Cabrillo Tide Pools State Marine Park, where you can observe fascinating marine life in their natural habitat. Point Loma is also home to the USS Midway Museum, where you can explore a retired aircraft carrier and learn about naval aviation history.

San Diego's neighborhoods offer a treasure trove of experiences waiting to be discovered. From the coastal beauty of La Jolla to the cultural diversity of Barrio Logan, each neighborhood adds its own unique flavor to the city.

Beaches and Water Activities

San Diego is a city with a rich history and culture, but it's also a city with a beautiful coastline. With over 70 miles of beaches to explore, there's something for everyone in San Diego, whether you're a surfer, a sunbather, or a water sports enthusiast.

Here are some of the best beaches and water activities to explore in San Diego:

Beaches

La Jolla Shores: This popular beach is known for its calm waters and beautiful scenery. It's also a great place to go snorkeling or diving, as there are several underwater caves and reefs to explore.

Pacific Beach: This lively beach is perfect for people-watching, swimming, and surfing. There are also plenty of bars and restaurants nearby, so you can easily make a day of it.

Mission Beach: This family-friendly beach is home to the world-famous Belmont Park amusement park. There are also several water parks and playgrounds nearby, making it a great place to take the kids.

Ocean Beach: This laid-back beach is known for its eclectic mix of shops, restaurants, and bars. It's also a great place to catch a sunset.

Coronado Beach: This beautiful beach is located on a peninsula just across the bay from

San Diego. It's a great place to go for a walk, have a picnic, or simply relax and enjoy the views.

Water Activities

Surfing: San Diego is a world-renowned surfing destination, with waves for all levels of experience. Some of the best surfing spots include La Jolla Shores, Pacific Beach, and Ocean Beach.

Bodyboarding: Bodyboarding is a great way to enjoy the waves without having to learn how to surf. There are several bodyboarding schools in San Diego that offer lessons for all levels of experience.

Kitesurfing: Kitesurfing is a thrilling water sport that combines elements of surfing, windsurfing, and paragliding. It's a great way to get some exercise and enjoy the views of the San Diego coastline.

Stand-up paddleboarding: Stand-up paddleboarding is a fun and easy way to explore the San Diego coastline. You can rent paddleboards from several places in San Diego, or bring your own.

Windsurfing: Windsurfing is a great way to combine the thrill of surfing with the power of the wind. It's a great way to get some exercise and enjoy the views of the San Diego coastline.

These are just a few of the many beaches and water activities to explore when on vacation in San Diego. With so much to offer, you're sure to find something to enjoy in this beautiful city.

Where To Eat and Drink

San Diego is a city with a diverse culinary scene, offering something for everyone. From casual eateries to fine dining establishments, there are plenty of great places to eat and drink in San Diego.

Here are a few of the best places to eat and drink when on vacation in San Diego:

George's at the Cove: This award-winning restaurant offers stunning views of the Pacific Ocean and a menu of creative seafood dishes.

The Oceanaire Seafood Room: This upscale restaurant is known for its fresh seafood and extensive wine list.

The Fish Market: This casual spot is a great place to enjoy fresh seafood tacos and margaritas.

Hodad's: This legendary burger joint has been serving up delicious burgers since 1954.

The Crack Shack: This farm-to-table restaurant specializes in fried chicken and other comfort foods.

The Patio: This outdoor restaurant is a great place to enjoy a meal with a view of the Gaslamp Quarter.

The Linkery: This gastropub offers a creative menu of small plates and craft beers.

The Polite Provisions: This cocktail bar is known for its creative cocktails and extensive whiskey selection.

The Nolen: This neighborhood bar is a great place to enjoy a craft beer or a glass of wine.

The Rabbit Hole: This speakeasy-style bar offers a unique dining experience and a wide selection of cocktails.

These are just a few of the many great places to eat and drink in San Diego. With so many options to choose from, you're sure to find the perfect place to enjoy a delicious meal or a refreshing drink.

Here are some additional tips for finding the best places to eat and drink in San Diego:

- Ask your hotel concierge for recommendations.

- Read online reviews of restaurants and bars.
- Check out social media for photos and reviews of local establishments.
- Visit popular tourist destinations, such as the Gaslamp Quarter and Little Italy, for a variety of dining options.
- Venture off the beaten path and explore some of San Diego's hidden gems.

With a little planning, you're sure to have a delicious and memorable dining experience in San Diego.

Accommodations in San Diego

San Diego is a beautiful city with a lot to offer visitors, from its stunning beaches to its world-class attractions. But with so many things to see and do, it can be tough to find a place to stay that's both affordable and nice. That's where this list comes in! Here are some great places to stay in San Diego that won't break the bank.

The Sofia Hotel

The Sofia Hotel is a boutique hotel located in the heart of the Gaslamp Quarter. It's a great choice for those who want to be close to all the action, and it offers a variety of amenities, including a rooftop pool, a fitness center, and a restaurant. Rooms start at around $150 per night.

The Gaslamp Hostel

The Gaslamp Hostel is a great option for budget-minded travelers. It's located in the heart of the Gaslamp Quarter, and it offers a variety of amenities, including a common area with a kitchen, a TV, and a game room. Dorm beds start at around $30 per night.

The Old Town Inn

The Old Town Inn is a historic hotel located in Old Town San Diego. It's a great choice for those who want to experience the city's rich history and culture. Rooms start at around $100 per night.

The Kings Inn

The Kings Inn is a budget-friendly hotel located near the airport. It's a great choice for those who want to be close to the airport, and it offers a variety of amenities, including a pool, a fitness center, and a free breakfast buffet. Rooms start at around $70 per night.

The Urban Boutique Hotel

The Urban Boutique Hotel is a stylish hotel located in the Gaslamp Quarter. It's a great choice for those who want to be close to all the action, and it offers a variety of amenities, including a rooftop pool, a fitness center, and a restaurant. Rooms start at around $175 per night.

The Best Western Plus Island Palms Hotel & Marina

The Best Western Plus Island Palms Hotel & Marina is a great option for those who want to be close to the water. It's located on Mission Bay, and it offers a variety of amenities, including a pool, a fitness center, and a marina. Rooms start at around $120 per night.

Surestay Hotel by Best Western - San Diego/pacific Beach

The Surestay Hotel by Best Western - San Diego/pacific Beach is a great option for those who want to be close to the beach. It's located in Pacific Beach, and it offers a variety of amenities, including a pool, a fitness center, and a free breakfast buffet. Rooms start at around $100 per night.

The Ocean Park Inn

The Ocean Park Inn is a charming bed and breakfast located in Ocean Beach. It's a great choice for those who want to experience the city's laid-back beach vibe. Rooms start at around $120 per night.

The Atwood Hotel

The Atwood Hotel is a stylish hotel located in the Gaslamp Quarter. It's a great choice for those who want to be close to all the action, and it offers a variety of amenities, including a rooftop pool, a fitness center, and a restaurant. Rooms start at around $200 per night.

The Hyatt Regency La Jolla at Aventine

The Hyatt Regency La Jolla at Aventine is a luxurious hotel located in La Jolla. It's a great choice for those who want to experience the city's upscale vibe. Rooms start at around $300 per night.

These are just a few of the many great places to stay in San Diego. With so many options to choose from, you're sure to find the perfect place to call home during your stay.

Here are some additional tips for finding affordable accommodation in San Diego:

- Book your stay in advance, especially if you're traveling during peak season.
- Look for hotels that offer discounts for AAA members, seniors, and military personnel.
- Consider staying in a hostel or bed and breakfast. These types of accommodations

are often more affordable than traditional hotels.

- Look for hotels that are located outside of the city center. These hotels are often less expensive than those located in the heart of the city.
- Take advantage of free amenities, such as breakfast buffets and pools. These amenities can save you money on food and entertainment.

With a little planning, you can easily find affordable accommodation in San Diego.

Shopping and Fashion

San Diego is a city with a diverse and vibrant shopping scene. Whether you're looking for high-end designer brands or unique finds, you'll find it all in San Diego.

Here are some of the best places to shop in San Diego:

Fashion Valley: This is San Diego's largest shopping mall, with over 200 stores, including Nordstrom, Neiman Marcus, Bloomingdale's, and Macy's. You'll also find a variety of restaurants and entertainment options at Fashion Valley.

Westfield UTC: This outdoor shopping center is located in La Jolla, and it's home to over 140 stores, including Anthropologie, J.Crew, and Banana Republic. There's also a movie theater and a food court at Westfield UTC.

Hillcrest: This vibrant neighborhood is known for its LGBTQ+ community, and it's also home to a number of unique boutiques and shops. You'll find everything from vintage clothing to home décor in Hillcrest.

Las Americas Premium Outlets: This outlet mall is located just across the border in Tijuana, Mexico, and it's home to over 150 designer stores, including Gucci, Louis Vuitton, and

Prada. You can save big on designer goods at Las Americas Premium Outlets.

Balboa Park: This world-famous park is home to 17 museums, as well as a number of shops and restaurants. You can find everything from souvenirs to art supplies at Balboa Park.

Seaport Village: This waterfront shopping and dining complex is located in downtown San Diego, and it's home to over 70 stores, restaurants, and bars. You can also catch a ferry to Coronado Island from Seaport Village.

Liberty Station: This former naval training station has been transformed into a vibrant mixed-use community, and it's home to a number of shops, restaurants, and art galleries. You can also find a farmers market at Liberty Station every Saturday.

Gaslamp Quarter: This historic district is home to over 160 shops, restaurants, and bars. You can find everything from vintage clothing to high-end fashion in the Gaslamp Quarter.

Old Town: This historic district is home to over 200 shops, restaurants, and museums. You can find everything from Mexican souvenirs to Native American crafts in Old Town.

No matter what your budget or style, you're sure to find something to love in San Diego.

132

Chapter 5: Exploring Orange County

Top Attractions in Orange County

Orange County boasts a kaleidoscope of attractions that cater to every interest and captivate all who visit. Whether you're a sun-seeking beach lover, a theme park enthusiast, a nature explorer, or a connoisseur of arts and culture, Orange County has something extraordinary to offer. Join us as we embark on a journey through the top attractions of this captivating county.

Stunning Beaches

Orange County is synonymous with idyllic beaches that leave visitors spellbound. From the iconic Huntington Beach, known as "Surf City USA," to the picturesque Laguna Beach with its pristine coves and dramatic cliffs, the coastal gems of Orange County offer endless opportunities for relaxation, water sports, and scenic strolls. Don't miss Newport Beach, famous for its harbor and Balboa Peninsula, and Crystal Cove State Park, a coastal paradise blending nature and history.

Disneyland Resort

The magical realm of Disneyland Resort needs no introduction. As Walt Disney's original theme park, it continues to enchant visitors of all ages. With two enchanting parks, Disneyland Park and Disney California Adventure Park, as well as Downtown Disney District, this iconic destination transports guests to a world of fantasy, thrilling rides, beloved characters, and unforgettable experiences. Immerse yourself in the magic and create memories to last a lifetime.

The Arts at Segerstrom Center for the Arts

Indulge your cultural cravings at the prestigious Segerstrom Center for the Arts in Costa Mesa. This world-class performing arts center showcases an array of captivating performances, including Broadway shows, ballets, symphonies, and contemporary dance. With its state-of-the-art facilities and renowned resident companies like Pacific Symphony and Pacific Chorale, the Segerstrom Center offers an exquisite cultural experience that will leave you awe-inspired.

Mission San Juan Capistrano

Step back in time and explore the rich historical tapestry of Orange County at Mission San Juan Capistrano. Founded in 1776, this iconic mission showcases Spanish colonial architecture and beautifully manicured gardens. Discover the fascinating history of the region, learn about the mission's role in early California, and witness the famous annual return of the swallows. The mission's serene atmosphere and intriguing exhibits make it a must-visit destination for history enthusiasts.

Crystal Cathedral

A true architectural marvel, the Crystal Cathedral in Garden Grove is a sight to behold. Also known as Christ Cathedral, this magnificent structure is an iconic landmark in Orange County. Admire the awe-inspiring design, featuring over 10,000 panes of glass, and explore the serene campus surrounding the cathedral. Attend a service, take a guided tour, or simply revel in the tranquility of this spiritual sanctuary.

Balboa Island

Escape to the charming island paradise of Balboa Island, located within Newport Beach. This enchanting coastal retreat offers a delightful blend of small-town charm, breathtaking waterfront views, and a range of recreational activities. Stroll along the picturesque Marine Avenue lined with boutique shops and tantalizing eateries. Rent a bike or kayak to explore the island's beauty or hop aboard the iconic Balboa Island Ferry for a scenic ride.

Discovery Cube Orange County

Ignite your curiosity and spark your imagination at the Discovery Cube Orange County. This interactive science center in Santa Ana offers an immersive learning experience for visitors of all ages. Engage in hands-on exhibits, explore the wonders of space, delve into the world of dinosaurs, and learn about sustainable living. With its focus on science, technology, engineering, and math (STEM) education, the Discovery Cube is both educational and entertaining, making it a perfect destination for families and curious minds.

Crystal Cove Historic District

Transport yourself to a bygone era as you wander through the Crystal Cove Historic District. This preserved coastal village, located within Crystal Cove State Park, showcases vintage beach cottages that evoke the charm of the 1920s and 1930s. Take a leisurely stroll along the sandy shoreline, explore the tide pools, or embark on a hike through the park's pristine wilderness. The district's nostalgic ambiance and stunning natural beauty make it a hidden gem within Orange County.

The Orange County Great Park

Situated on the former grounds of the El Toro Marine Corps Air Station, the Orange County Great Park is a sprawling recreational space that offers something for everyone. This 1,300-acre park features sports fields, picnic areas, a carousel, a farmers market, and even a tethered helium balloon that provides panoramic views of the surrounding area. Enjoy outdoor activities, attend community events, or simply relish the tranquil beauty of this expansive park.

Orange County Museum of Art

Art enthusiasts will find a haven at the Orange County Museum of Art (OCMA) in Santa Ana.

This vibrant institution showcases a diverse collection of contemporary and modern art from both local and international artists. Explore thought-provoking exhibitions, participate in engaging programs, and experience the dynamic world of visual arts. The museum's commitment to fostering creativity and innovation makes it a captivating destination for art lovers.

Irvine Regional Park

Escape the hustle and bustle of city life and immerse yourself in nature at Irvine Regional Park. Located in the heart of Orange County, this expansive park offers a myriad of outdoor activities and recreational opportunities. Explore the scenic hiking and biking trails, take a leisurely ride on the park's famous Orange County Zoo Railroad, or enjoy a picnic amidst the park's lush surroundings. With its serene ambiance and abundant wildlife, Irvine Regional Park is a peaceful retreat for nature enthusiasts.

Knott's Berry Farm

Thrill-seekers and amusement park enthusiasts will find their adrenaline fix at Knott's Berry Farm. This iconic theme park, located in Buena Park, features an exciting array of roller coasters, live entertainment, and family-friendly attractions. Embark on heart-pounding rides, witness thrilling shows, and indulge in the park's famous boysenberry treats. With its rich history and exciting atmosphere, Knott's Berry Farm promises an unforgettable adventure for visitors of all ages.

Orange County's top attractions offer an enticing blend of natural beauty, cultural richness, and exhilarating experiences. Whether you're soaking up the sun on the golden beaches, exploring the region's history and art, immersing yourself in the world of Disney magic, or enjoying the tranquility of nature, Orange County is a destination that promises to captivate and delight. So, embark on an unforgettable journey and discover the remarkable charms of this Southern Californian gem.

Best Neighborhoods To Explore

Orange County, California, is a sun-soaked paradise that offers an abundance of attractions and experiences for every type of traveler. From stunning beaches and world-class shopping to eclectic dining and outdoor adventures, Orange County has it all. To make the most of your visit, let's explore the best neighborhoods this picturesque region has to offer. So grab your sunscreen and sense of adventure as we embark on a journey to discover the top neighborhoods in Orange County.

Laguna Beach

Nestled along the Pacific Ocean, Laguna Beach is a haven for art lovers and nature enthusiasts. Stroll through the charming streets lined with art galleries, boutiques, and vibrant cafes. Don't miss a visit to the Laguna Art Museum, showcasing California artists. Enjoy the breathtaking coastline by exploring the pristine beaches or hiking the scenic trails of Crystal Cove State Park. End your day by catching a mesmerizing sunset over the ocean.

Newport Beach

For those seeking a mix of luxury, outdoor activities, and coastal charm, Newport Beach is a must-visit. Spend the day exploring Balboa Island, known for its quaint shops, waterfront dining, and the iconic Balboa Fun Zone. Take a harbor cruise or rent a boat to experience the beauty of Newport Bay. For beach lovers, Newport Beach's expansive coastline offers great opportunities for surfing, sunbathing, or simply relaxing by the waves.

Downtown Fullerton

Experience the vibrant energy of Orange County's diverse music and arts scene in Downtown Fullerton. The lively streets are brimming with indie boutiques, hipster coffee shops, and trendy restaurants. Music enthusiasts can catch live performances at The Continental Room or check out the latest art exhibits at the Magoski Arts Colony. Don't miss a visit to the historic Fox Theatre, a beautifully restored venue hosting a variety of entertainment events.

Anaheim

Home to the world-famous Disneyland Resort, Anaheim is a destination that appeals to the young and the young at heart. Spend a day exploring the enchanting Disneyland Park or the neighboring Disney California Adventure Park. For sports lovers, catch an electrifying game at the Angel Stadium or visit the Honda Center for hockey or concerts. Discover culinary delights at the Anaheim Packing District, a food hall featuring a wide range of cuisines.

Huntington Beach

Known as "Surf City, USA," Huntington Beach offers an authentic California beach experience. The iconic Huntington Beach Pier is a perfect spot for panoramic ocean views, surfing, and people-watching. Visit the International Surfing Museum to learn about the history and culture of this beloved sport. Explore the vibrant downtown area, Main Street, filled with surf shops, unique boutiques, and inviting restaurants.

Orange County's diverse neighborhoods offer a plethora of experiences to satisfy any traveler's wanderlust. From the artistic charm of Laguna Beach to the coastal luxury of Newport Beach, each neighborhood has its own unique character and attractions.

Where To Eat and Drink

Whether you're a foodie or simply looking to indulge in delicious cuisine during your visit, Orange County has an array of dining options that will delight your taste buds. From fine dining establishments to casual eateries, here's a curated list of the best places to eat and drink as a tourist in Orange County.

The Deck on Laguna Beach (Laguna Beach)

Located right on the sandy shores of Laguna Beach, The Deck offers a breathtaking oceanfront dining experience. Enjoy a refreshing cocktail while savoring the fresh seafood menu.

The relaxed atmosphere, stunning views, and exceptional cuisine make it a must-visit for both locals and tourists.

Playground (Santa Ana)

If you're seeking an innovative and ever-changing dining experience, Playground is the place to be. This trendy restaurant features a seasonal menu that highlights local and sustainable ingredients. The chef's culinary creativity shines through in dishes that are both visually stunning and bursting with flavor.

Habana (Costa Mesa)

Transport yourself to the vibrant streets of Havana at Habana, a Cuban-inspired restaurant located in the heart of Costa Mesa. The restaurant's stunning architecture, lively atmosphere, and authentic cuisine create an immersive dining experience. Indulge in classic dishes like Ropa Vieja and Mojitos while enjoying live music and a vibrant ambiance.

Broadway by Amar Santana (Laguna Beach)

Broadway is a fine dining gem nestled in Laguna Beach, offering a culinary journey through modern American cuisine. Chef Amar Santana's innovative dishes showcase his mastery of flavors and presentation. The restaurant's sleek and contemporary setting provides an elegant backdrop for a memorable dining experience.

Bosscat Kitchen & Libations (Newport Beach)

For whiskey enthusiasts and comfort food lovers, Bosscat Kitchen and Libations is a must-visit destination. With an impressive collection of over 300 whiskeys, this gastropub offers an extensive menu featuring elevated American classics. Don't miss their signature whiskey-infused desserts, such as the Bourbon Bread Pudding.

The Anaheim Packing House (Anaheim)

Steeped in history and filled with culinary delights, the Anaheim Packing House is a food lover's paradise. This restored citrus packing house is home to a diverse collection of food stalls and artisanal eateries, offering cuisines from around the world. From gourmet burgers to Vietnamese pho, there's something to please every palate.

A Restaurant (Newport Beach)

For a taste of classic steakhouse elegance, head to A Restaurant in Newport Beach. This iconic establishment has been a local favorite since 1926. Indulge in prime steaks, fresh seafood, and an extensive wine list in a sophisticated setting. The timeless ambiance and impeccable service create a memorable dining experience.

The Winery Restaurant & Wine Bar (Tustin)

The Winery is a culinary haven for wine lovers, offering an extensive selection of wines from around the world. The menu features seasonal and locally sourced ingredients, crafted into delectable dishes. The elegant setting, knowledgeable staff, and exceptional wine pairings make this restaurant a true gem.

Orange County boasts an impressive culinary scene, catering to all tastes and preferences. Whether you're seeking beachfront dining, international flavors, or fine dining experiences, this list highlights some of the best places to eat and drink as a tourist in Orange County. Embrace the diverse flavors, vibrant ambiance, and exceptional hospitality that this Southern California destination has to offer, and prepare for a culinary adventure you won't soon forget.

Accommodations in Orange County

With so much to see and do, it's no wonder that Orange County is a popular vacation spot. If you're planning a trip to Orange County, you'll need to find a place to stay. There are a variety of accommodation options available, from budget-friendly motels to luxurious resorts.

Here are some nice and affordable accommodation options to stay in Orange County:

The Anaheim Majestic Garden Hotel

The Anaheim Majestic Garden Hotel is a great option for budget-minded travelers who want to be close to all the action. This hotel is located just a short walk from Disneyland and the Anaheim Convention Center, and it offers a variety of amenities, including a pool, fitness center, and free Wi-Fi. Rooms start at around $100 per night.

The Howard Johnson by Wyndham Anaheim Hotel and Water Playground

The Howard Johnson by Wyndham Anaheim Hotel and Water Playground is another great option for families on a budget. This hotel features a water playground, pool, and hot tub, as well as a free breakfast buffet. Rooms start at around $90 per night.

The Capri Laguna on the Beach

The Capri Laguna on the Beach is a charming boutique hotel located in the heart of Laguna Beach. This hotel offers stunning views of the

Pacific Ocean, as well as a private beach, pool, and hot tub. Rooms start at around $150 per night.

The Ayres Hotel Anaheim

The Ayres Hotel Anaheim is a great option for business travelers who want to be close to the Anaheim Convention Center. This hotel offers a variety of amenities, including a pool, fitness center, and free Wi-Fi. Rooms start at around $120 per night.

The Cortona Inn & Suites Anaheim Resort

The Cortona Inn & Suites Anaheim Resort is a great option for families who want to be close to Disneyland. This hotel features a pool, hot tub, and free breakfast buffet. Rooms start at around $130 per night.

The SpringHill Suites by Marriott Anaheim Maingate

The SpringHill Suites by Marriott Anaheim Maingate is a great option for business travelers who want to be close to the Disneyland Resort.

This hotel offers a variety of amenities, including a pool, fitness center, and free Wi-Fi. Rooms start at around $140 per night.

The SunCoast Park Hotel, Tapestry Collection by Hilton

The SunCoast Park Hotel, Tapestry Collection by Hilton is a great option for travelers who want to be close to the Anaheim Convention Center. This hotel offers a pool, fitness center, and free Wi-Fi. Rooms start at around $150 per night.

The Grand Legacy At The Park

The Grand Legacy At The Park is a great option for travelers who want to be close to the Disneyland Resort. This hotel offers a pool, fitness center, and free Wi-Fi. Rooms start at around $160 per night.

The Hyatt Place at Anaheim Resort/Convention Center

The Hyatt Place at Anaheim Resort/Convention Center is a great option for business travelers who want to be close to the Anaheim Convention Center. This hotel offers a pool, fitness center, and free Wi-Fi. Rooms start at around $170 per night.

The La Casa del Camino

The La Casa del Camino is a charming bed and breakfast located in the heart of Old Town Orange. This hotel offers a pool, hot tub, and free Wi-Fi. Rooms start at around $180 per night.

Directions

All of the hotels listed above are located in the heart of Orange County, making them easily accessible by car, bus, or train.

By Car

To get to Orange County from Los Angeles, take the I-5 Freeway south. To get to Orange County from San Diego, take the I-5 Freeway north.

By Bus

There are several bus companies that offer service to Orange County, including Greyhound and Amtrak.

By Train
The Metrolink Orange County Line offers service to Orange County from Los Angeles and San Diego.

I hope this list of affordable accommodation options helps you plan your trip to Orange County.

Shopping and Fashion

Orange County is a shopper's paradise, with everything from high-end boutiques to outlet malls to flea markets. Whether you're looking for a new outfit for a special occasion or just want to browse for some new treasures, you're sure to find it in Orange County.

Here are some of the best places to shop in Orange County:

South Coast Plaza: is one of the largest and most luxurious shopping malls in the United States. It's home to over 250 stores, including all of the top designer brands.

Fashion Island: is another upscale shopping destination, located in Newport Beach. It features over 200 stores, as well as a variety of restaurants and cafes.

The Irvine Spectrum Center: is a more casual shopping mall, with over 150 stores, including a movie theater and an ice skating rink.

The Outlets at Orange: is a great place to find designer brands at discounted prices. It features over 120 stores, including Nordstrom Rack, Banana Republic Factory Store, and Coach Outlet.

The Shops at Mission Viejo: is a family-friendly shopping center with over 150 stores, as well as a variety of restaurants and entertainment options.

In addition to these major shopping destinations, there are also a number of smaller boutiques and specialty shops throughout Orange County. Whether you're looking for vintage clothing, handmade jewelry, or locally-made goods, you're sure to find it in Orange County.

Here are a few tips for shopping in Orange County:

- Plan your trip ahead of time. If you're looking for something specific, it's a good idea to do some research before you go. That way, you can make sure you don't miss out on any of your favorite stores.

- Bring comfortable shoes. You're going to do a lot of walking, so make sure you're wearing shoes that you can move around in.

- Pack a bag. You're bound to find some great deals, so it's a good idea to bring a bag to carry your purchases.

- Don't be afraid to bargain. Many stores are willing to negotiate prices, so don't be afraid to ask.
- Take advantage of the sales. Many stores have sales throughout the year, so be sure to check the calendar before you go.

- Enjoy yourself. Shopping should be fun, so relax and take your time. There's no need to rush.

With so many great places to shop, Orange County is the perfect place to find something new for your wardrobe.

Coastal Attractions

Orange County is a coastal county in Southern California, known for its beautiful beaches, sunny weather, and laid-back lifestyle. There are many coastal attractions in Orange County to enjoy, from world-renowned surfing spots to charming seaside towns.

One of the most popular coastal attractions in Orange County is Huntington Beach, also known as "Surf City USA." Huntington Beach is home to some of the best surfing in the world, and it's also a great place to sunbathe, swim, and bodyboard. The Huntington Beach Pier is a popular spot for fishing, and there are also many shops and restaurants located along the pier.

Another popular coastal attraction in Orange County is Laguna Beach. Laguna Beach is a charming town with beautiful beaches, art galleries, and boutiques. There are also many hiking trails in the hills above Laguna Beach, which offer stunning views of the coastline.

Crystal Cove State Park is a beautiful coastal park located between Newport Beach and Laguna Beach. The park has miles of hiking trails, tide pools, and historic cottages. Crystal Cove State Park is a great place to relax and enjoy the natural beauty of Orange County.

Balboa Island is a charming island located in Newport Beach. The island has a quaint downtown area with shops, restaurants, and art galleries. Balboa Island is also home to the Balboa Fun Zone, an amusement park with rides, games, and food.

These are just a few of the many coastal attractions in Orange County. With its beautiful beaches, sunny weather, and laid-back lifestyle, Orange County is the perfect place to relax and enjoy the California coast.

Here are some additional tips for planning your trip to Orange County:

- The best time to visit Orange County is during the spring (March-May) or fall (September-November) when the weather is mild.

- If you're planning on spending a lot of time at the beach, be sure to pack sunscreen, a hat, and sunglasses.

- There are many different ways to get around Orange County, including by car, bus, train, and ferry.

- Be sure to check the local weather forecast before you go, as the weather can change quickly in Southern California.

- Orange County is a great place to visit with kids, as there are many family-friendly activities and attractions.

- Be sure to try some of the local cuisine, such as fish tacos, poke bowls, and In-N-Out Burger.

- Orange County is a great place to relax and unwind, so be sure to take some time to enjoy the beautiful scenery and laid-back lifestyle.

Chapter 6: Exploring Palm Springs and the Desert

Top attractions in Palm Springs

Palm Springs is a desert oasis in Southern California, known for its warm weather, stunning scenery, and vibrant arts and culture scene. Whether you're looking to relax by the pool, hike in the mountains, or explore the city's many museums and galleries, there's something for everyone in Palm Springs.

Here are some of the Top Attractions in Palm Springs:

Palm Springs Aerial Tramway: This iconic tram takes visitors up to Mount San Jacinto, offering stunning views of the Coachella Valley and the surrounding mountains.

Indian Canyons: These three canyons are home to the Agua Caliente Band of Cahuilla Indians, and offer stunning scenery and hiking trails.

Palm Springs Art Museum: This museum features a collection of modern and contemporary art, as well as rotating exhibits.

Palm Springs Air Museum: This museum houses a collection of vintage aircraft, including World War II bombers and fighters.

Living Desert Zoo and Gardens: This zoo and gardens features animals from all over the world, as well as a variety of gardens and exhibits.

Coachella Valley Preserve: This 1,200-acre preserve protects a variety of desert habitats, including sand dunes, washes, and mountains.

VillageFest: This weekly outdoor market features arts and crafts, food, and live music.

Elvis Honeymoon Hideaway: This historic home was once the honeymoon destination of Elvis and Priscilla Presley.

Sunnylands: This estate was once the home of Walter and Leonore Annenberg, and is now a museum and cultural center.

Hobart Lowe House: This mid century modern home is now a museum and event space.

These are just a few of the many things to see and do in Palm Springs. With its warm weather, stunning scenery, and vibrant culture, Palm Springs is the perfect place to relax, explore, and have fun.

Here are some additional tips for planning your trip to Palm Springs:

- The best time to visit Palm Springs is during the spring (March-May) or fall (September-November) when the weather is mild.

- Palm Springs is a popular destination, so it's important to book your accommodations and activities in advance, especially if you're traveling during peak season.

- Palm Springs is a walkable city, but you'll also want to rent a car if you plan on exploring the surrounding area.

- There are a variety of dining options in Palm Springs, from casual cafes to fine dining restaurants.

- Palm Springs is a great place to relax and unwind, but there are also plenty of activities to keep you busy. Be sure to check out the city's many museums, galleries, and shops.

- Palm Springs is a welcoming city, and everyone is sure to find something to enjoy.

Best Neighborhoods To Explore

Nestled in the picturesque Coachella Valley, Palm Springs is a desert oasis that has captivated travelers for decades. Known for its year-round sunshine, stunning mountain vistas, and mid-century modern architecture, this vibrant city offers a myriad of neighborhoods, each with its own unique charm.

Historic Tennis Club

Let's begin our adventure in the heart of Palm Springs at the Historic Tennis Club neighborhood. This historic district showcases the city's rich heritage and boasts a collection of charming boutique hotels, intimate restaurants, and art galleries. Stroll down the iconic Palm Canyon Drive, soak in the old-world ambiance, and explore the hidden gems nestled within its winding streets. Don't miss the chance to visit the Palm Springs Art Museum and immerse yourself in the vibrant local art scene.

Movie Colony

Prepare to step back in time as we venture into the Movie Colony, where Hollywood's golden era comes to life. This neighborhood was once a haven for movie stars seeking respite from the bustling city. Today, it retains its glamorous allure with meticulously preserved estates and palm-lined streets. Take a leisurely walk along the Movie Colony Loop, where you'll be enthralled by the architectural masterpieces that once housed legendary icons. The Movie Colony is also home to the Palm Springs Walk of Stars, paying homage to the stars of yesteryears.

Uptown Design District

For the art and design enthusiasts, the Uptown Design District is an absolute must-visit. This creative hub boasts an array of eclectic boutiques, antique shops, and contemporary art galleries. Explore the Palm Springs Modernism architecture, characterized by sleek lines and innovative designs, and delve into the world of mid-century modern furniture at the various specialty stores. Satisfy your taste buds at the trendy cafes and gourmet restaurants that line the streets, offering a delightful fusion of flavors.

Tahquitz River Estates

Nature lovers, rejoice! The Tahquitz River Estates neighborhood is a paradise for outdoor enthusiasts. Bordered by the majestic San Jacinto Mountains, this serene area is known for its hiking trails, tranquil parks, and lush greenery. Embark on a scenic hike through the Indian Canyons or relax by the Tahquitz Creek, immersing yourself in the natural beauty that surrounds you. Don't forget to keep an eye out for the diverse wildlife that calls this area home.

El Paseo

Indulge in a luxurious shopping and dining experience at El Paseo, often referred to as the "Rodeo Drive of the Desert." This upscale neighborhood offers an array of high-end boutiques, renowned art galleries, and exquisite restaurants. Take a leisurely stroll down the palm-lined street, marvel at the stunning displays of art, and treat yourself to a gourmet meal at one of the many acclaimed eateries. El Paseo also hosts various cultural events throughout the year, including art festivals and fashion shows.

Deepwell Estates

As we venture into Deepwell Estates, prepare to be captivated by the allure of the desert's tranquil lifestyle. Known for its sprawling estates and lush gardens, this exclusive neighborhood showcases the epitome of desert living. Explore the architectural marvels that blend seamlessly with the natural landscape and enjoy the serenity that envelops this secluded enclave. For a glimpse into the local history, visit the Deepwell Estates Historic District and discover the stories behind the charming mid-century homes.

Palm Springs is a captivating destination that offers an abundance of diverse neighborhoods, each with its own distinct character and appeal. From the historic charm of the Tennis Club to the glitz and glamor of the Movie Colony, the artistic energy of the Uptown Design District, the natural beauty of Tahquitz River Estates, the luxury of El Paseo, and the tranquil oasis of Deepwell Estates, there is something for every traveler to discover and enjoy.

In addition to the unique atmosphere and attractions of each neighborhood, Palm Springs offers a wealth of activities and experiences that further enhance your visit. Indulge in the rejuvenating power of the city's renowned spas, play a round of golf at one of the many world-class courses, or embark on a thrilling adventure with hot air ballooning, horseback riding, or off-road excursions in the nearby desert.

Palm Springs is also famous for its vibrant cultural scene. Don't miss the opportunity to attend one of the city's many festivals and events, such as the Palm Springs International Film Festival or the Modernism Week, which celebrates the mid-century modern architecture that defines the region. Immerse yourself in the local art and music scene by exploring the numerous galleries, attending live performances, or visiting the Palm Springs Art Museum.

When it comes to dining, Palm Springs is a food lover's paradise. From upscale restaurants offering gourmet cuisine to casual eateries serving mouthwatering dishes, the city's culinary scene is diverse and exciting. Sample the flavors of the desert with dishes featuring fresh ingredients like dates, citrus fruits, and locally sourced produce. Don't forget to try the iconic palm-inspired cocktails that have become synonymous with Palm Springs' laid-back sophistication.

As you explore the neighborhoods of Palm Springs, it's essential to make the most of the city's abundant sunshine and pleasant climate. Take advantage of the beautiful weather by enjoying outdoor activities like hiking, biking, or simply lounging by the pool. The stunning backdrop of the San Jacinto Mountains provides the perfect setting for outdoor adventures and breathtaking views.

When planning your visit to Palm Springs, it's worth considering the city's diverse events calendar and the availability of accommodations in each neighborhood. Whether you prefer luxury resorts, charming boutique hotels, or vacation rentals, Palm Springs offers a range of options to suit every taste and budget. Each neighborhood has its own selection of accommodations, allowing you to immerse yourself fully in the distinctive ambiance of your chosen area.

Palm Springs is a destination that offers much more than meets the eye. Its neighborhoods are vibrant, unique, and captivating, each offering a different experience and atmosphere. Whether you're drawn to history, architecture, art, nature, luxury, or relaxation, Palm Springs has it all. So, pack your bags, put on your sunglasses, and get ready to embark on a memorable journey through the best neighborhoods this desert paradise has to offer.

Where To Eat and Drink

Welcome to Orange County, a vibrant and diverse culinary paradise that offers a wide range of dining experiences to satisfy every palate. From charming beachside cafes to upscale fine dining establishments, Orange County has something for everyone. Join us on a culinary journey as we explore the best places to eat and drink in this enchanting region of Southern California.

The Playground - Santa Ana

Located in Santa Ana's Downtown, The Playground is a food lover's dream. Led by renowned chef Jason Quinn, this gastropub boasts a seasonal menu that showcases the freshest locally sourced ingredients. The ever-changing menu offers an adventurous blend of flavors, with dishes like duck fat fries, crispy pork belly, and inventive desserts. The intimate ambiance and knowledgeable staff make dining at The Playground an unforgettable experience.

Marché Moderne - Newport Beach

Indulge in French culinary excellence at Marché Moderne, a Michelin-starred restaurant in Newport Beach. The husband-and-wife team, Florent and Amelia Marneau, bring their passion for French cuisine to life with their menu. From delicate foie gras and perfectly cooked seafood to decadent desserts, Marché Moderne offers a sophisticated dining experience in an elegant setting.

Habana - Costa Mesa

Transport yourself to Havana at Habana, a Cuban-inspired restaurant located in Costa Mesa. The vibrant atmosphere, complete with lush foliage and live music, sets the stage for an unforgettable dining experience. Feast on traditional Cuban dishes like ropa vieja, lechon asado, and delectable empanadas. Pair your meal with a refreshing mojito or a handcrafted cocktail from their extensive drink menu.

Anepalco - Orange

Discover the unique flavors of Mexican-French fusion cuisine at Anepalco, a hidden gem located in the city of Orange. Led by Chef Daniel Godinez, this innovative restaurant combines traditional Mexican ingredients with French culinary techniques. Try their famous chilaquiles, made with a twist, or the mouthwatering duck confit enchiladas. The brunch menu is equally enticing, featuring dishes like the decadent Nutella stuffed French toast.

The Winery Restaurant & Wine Bar - Newport Beach

For wine enthusiasts, The Winery Restaurant & Wine Bar in Newport Beach is a must-visit. This upscale establishment offers a remarkable selection of wines from around the world, expertly paired with an exquisite menu. From prime steaks and fresh seafood to artisanal cheese and charcuterie boards, The Winery guarantees an elevated dining experience accompanied by impeccable service.

Bear Flag Fish Co. - Newport Beach

For seafood lovers, Bear Flag Fish Co. is a true gem nestled in Newport Beach. This casual eatery serves up fresh, high-quality seafood, sourced directly from local fishermen. Whether you're in the mood for a mouthwatering fish taco, a hearty seafood platter, or a refreshing poke bowl, Bear Flag Fish Co. delivers on taste, freshness, and value.

Sidecar Doughnuts & Coffee - Costa Mesa

Satisfy your sweet tooth with a visit to Sidecar Doughnuts & Coffee in Costa Mesa. This artisanal doughnut shop takes the humble doughnut to new heights with its creative flavors and made-from-scratch approach. Indulge in their signature huckleberry doughnut or explore rotating seasonal offerings like maple bacon or earl grey. Pair your doughnut with a perfectly brewed cup of coffee for a delightful treat.

The Iron Press - Anaheim

Calling all beer and waffle enthusiasts! The Iron Press in Anaheim is the perfect spot to enjoy a unique culinary experience. This gastropub specializes in gourmet waffle sandwiches and an extensive selection of craft beers. Indulge in their famous Chicken and Waffle sandwich or explore their inventive creations like the Monte Cristo Waffle. With a laid-back atmosphere and a rotating lineup of beers on tap, The Iron Press is a favorite among locals and visitors alike.

Break of Dawn - Laguna Hills

For a truly memorable breakfast or brunch experience, head to Break of Dawn in Laguna Hills. Chef Dee Nguyen's innovative approach to breakfast cuisine has earned this small, unassuming restaurant a loyal following. Expect dishes that blend Asian, American, and European influences, such as the Vietnamese Shrimp and Grits or the indulgent Caramelized Banana Pancakes. The use of locally sourced ingredients and Chef Dee's passion for culinary excellence make Break of Dawn a hidden gem.

Puesto - Irvine

Craving authentic Mexican street tacos? Look no further than Puesto in Irvine. This vibrant taqueria takes taco enjoyment to new heights with their creative and flavorful combinations. From their signature filet mignon taco to the refreshing Baja fish taco, each bite is a burst of authentic Mexican flavors. Don't forget to pair your tacos with one of their handcrafted margaritas for the ultimate culinary experience.

Arc - Costa Mesa

Located in the heart of Costa Mesa, Arc is a true haven for meat lovers. The restaurant's centerpiece is a custom-made wood-burning oven, which imparts a smoky flavor to their carefully sourced meats and seasonal vegetables. Indulge in dishes like the bone-in ribeye, wood-roasted chicken, or the succulent dry-aged pork chop. With its rustic ambiance and commitment to sustainable ingredients, Arc is a must-visit for carnivores.

Shuck Oyster Bar - Costa Mesa

If you're a fan of seafood and oysters, Shuck Oyster Bar in Costa Mesa is a paradise for you. This cozy and intimate eatery offers a wide selection of fresh oysters sourced from both coasts. Whether you prefer them raw or grilled, Shuck Oyster Bar serves them with precision and artistry. Pair your oysters with their tasty seafood chowder or indulge in their lobster roll for a truly satisfying meal.

The Blind Rabbit - Anaheim

For a unique and immersive dining experience, step into The Blind Rabbit, a hidden speakeasy located in Anaheim. This prohibition-era-inspired establishment offers craft cocktails and a menu of small plates designed to tantalize your taste buds. To gain entry, you'll need a secret password, adding to the sense of exclusivity and adventure. From the innovative libations to the meticulous attention to detail, The Blind Rabbit transports you to a bygone era of clandestine indulgence.

Baja Fish Tacos - Multiple Locations

No culinary journey through Orange County would be complete without indulging in the region's iconic fish tacos. Baja Fish Tacos has several locations throughout the county, offering a taste of Baja California's vibrant street food scene. Enjoy generous portions of crispy fish or shrimp, topped with fresh cabbage, salsa, and a squeeze of lime. The authentic flavors and casual atmosphere make Baja Fish Tacos a beloved local favorite.

Orange County's culinary landscape is a testament to its cultural diversity and commitment to culinary excellence. From Michelin-starred establishments to hidden gems and casual eateries, the region offers an array of dining options to suit every taste and occasion.

Accommodations in Palm Springs

Here are some nice and affordable accommodation options to consider when visiting Palm Springs. Each option includes the approximate price range per night and directions to locate the place:

The Saguaro Palm Springs

Situated in the vibrant Uptown Design District, The Saguaro offers a colorful and lively atmosphere. With rates ranging from $100 to $150 per night, it's a budget-friendly option. To find it, head towards 1800 E Palm Canyon Dr, Palm Springs, CA 92264.

Palm Springs Rendezvous

This charming boutique hotel offers a retro-themed experience with affordable rates ranging from $120 to $180 per night. It's located at 1420 N Indian Canyon Dr, Palm Springs, CA 92262, providing easy access to downtown Palm Springs.

Alcazar Palm Springs

Nestled in the popular Palm Springs Art District, Alcazar offers a trendy yet budget-friendly stay. With rates ranging from $150 to $200 per night, you can find it at 622 N Palm Canyon Dr, Palm Springs, CA 92262.

The Triangle Inn

For a unique and LGBTQ-friendly experience, The Triangle Inn is a cozy clothing-optional resort. Rates range from $130 to $180 per night. To locate it, head towards 555 E San Lorenzo Rd, Palm Springs, CA 92264.

Del Marcos Hotel

This mid-century modern hotel offers a chic and stylish ambiance. Prices range from $150 to $250 per night. You can find it at 225 W Baristo Rd, Palm Springs, CA 92262, near downtown Palm Springs.

Caliente Tropics Hotel

Ideal for those seeking a retro-themed stay, Caliente Tropics Hotel offers affordable rates ranging from $100 to $150 per night. It's located at 411 E Palm Canyon Dr, Palm Springs, CA 92264.

Ingleside Inn

This historic boutique hotel offers a classic Palm Springs experience. With rates ranging from $200 to $300 per night, it's located at 200 W Ramon Rd, Palm Springs, CA 92264, near downtown Palm Springs.

Vagabond Inn Palm Springs

Conveniently situated on the outskirts of Palm Springs, Vagabond Inn offers affordable rates starting from $80 to $120 per night. To locate it, head towards 1699 S Palm Canyon Dr, Palm Springs, CA 92264.

Skylark Hotel

A mid-century modern gem, Skylark Hotel offers affordable rates ranging from $120 to $180 per night. You can find it at 1466 N Palm Canyon Dr, Palm Springs, CA 92262.

Ivy Palm Resort & Spa

For a budget-friendly option with added amenities, Ivy Palm Resort & Spa offers rates ranging from $100 to $150 per night. It's located at 2000 N Palm Canyon Dr, Palm Springs, CA 92262.

Remember to check the specific rates and availability for your desired dates, as prices may vary depending on the season and any ongoing promotions.

Shopping and Fashion

For fashion-forward travelers, Palm Springs is a true shopping paradise, boasting an array of unique boutiques, upscale retailers, and vintage treasure troves. Here, we'll delve into everything you need to know about shopping and fashion in Palm Springs, ensuring you make the most of your retail therapy while immersing yourself in the city's distinctive charm.

The Palm Springs Shopping Experience

When it comes to shopping, Palm Springs caters to every taste and style, creating an eclectic mix of modern and vintage treasures. The city's main shopping areas are Downtown Palm Springs, El

Paseo, and the Uptown Design District. Each district has its own distinct character, offering an unparalleled retail experience.

a. Downtown Palm Springs

Stroll along Palm Canyon Drive and Palm Springs' main shopping street, where you'll find a myriad of shops ranging from high-end boutiques to art galleries and trendy home decor stores. This bustling strip is perfect for fashion enthusiasts looking for contemporary styles, designer labels, and unique accessories.

b. El Paseo

Known as the "Rodeo Drive of the Desert," El Paseo is Palm Springs' premier luxury shopping destination. This upscale mile-long stretch is home to internationally renowned fashion brands, exclusive designer boutiques, and high-end galleries. Indulge in a shopping spree surrounded by palm-lined streets, and don't forget to explore the exquisite art installations scattered along the avenue.

c. Uptown Design District

For the fashion-forward individual seeking one-of-a-kind vintage finds, Uptown Design District is a must-visit. This vibrant neighborhood is brimming with retro-inspired clothing stores, antique shops, and independent designers showcasing their eclectic creations. Immerse yourself in the spirit of Palm Springs' mid-century modern architecture while uncovering unique fashion gems.

Unleashing Palm Springs' Fashion Scene

Palm Springs is not only a shopping destination but also a vibrant hub for fashion enthusiasts. Throughout the year, the city hosts various fashion events, making it an ideal place to witness the latest trends, discover emerging designers, and engage in the fashion community.

a. Palm Springs International Fashion Week

Plan your visit around November to witness the Palm Springs International Fashion Week, a grand event that showcases collections from both established and emerging designers. The week-long extravaganza includes runway shows, pop-up shops, and exclusive after-parties, providing a comprehensive look into the fashion world.

b. Trina Turk Boutique

No visit to Palm Springs would be complete without exploring the iconic Trina Turk Boutique. Known for its vibrant colors, bold prints, and chic resort wear, Trina Turk's flagship store beautifully captures the essence of Palm Springs' vibrant and stylish atmosphere.

c. Vintage Shopping:

Palm Springs has a rich history deeply intertwined with mid-century modern design, and the city proudly preserves its vintage charm. Visit renowned vintage stores such as The Frippery and Modernway, where you can discover authentic clothing and accessories from the golden era of Palm Springs' fashion.

Embracing Palm Springs' Desert Chic

Palm Springs' unique climate and desert setting have given birth to a distinctive style known as "Desert Chic." This fashion trend celebrates a fusion of relaxed resort wear, vibrant colors, and modern design elements. To fully embrace the Palm Springs fashion scene, consider the following style tips:

a. Light and Airy Fabrics:
Opt for lightweight, breathable fabrics such as linen, cotton, and silk to stay comfortable in Palm Springs' warm climate. Flowy maxi dresses, breezy tops, and linen pants are perfect choices for both style and comfort.

b. Vibrant Colors and Prints:
Palm Springs is all about embracing bold and vibrant colors. Incorporate vibrant hues like turquoise, coral, and lemon yellow into your wardrobe. Don't shy away from playful prints like palm leaves, geometric patterns, and retro motifs that reflect the city's energetic spirit.

c. Statement Accessories:

Accessorize your outfits with statement pieces that capture the essence of Palm Springs. Wide-brimmed hats, oversized sunglasses, colorful scarves, and chunky jewelry can add a touch of glamour and complete your desert chic look.

d. Footwear:
Opt for comfortable footwear as you explore the city's vibrant streets and shops. Sandals, espadrilles, and lightweight sneakers are excellent choices for walking while keeping your style on point.

Local Artisanal and Eco-Friendly Fashion

Palm Springs has a thriving community of local artisans and designers who specialize in sustainable and eco-friendly fashion. Discover unique and ethically-made pieces that contribute to a more conscious shopping experience. Explore boutiques like the Desert X Shop, featuring limited-edition collaborations with artists inspired by the desert landscape.

Insider Tips for the Ultimate Shopping Experience:

a. Timing: Consider visiting Palm Springs during the weekdays to avoid crowds and have a more relaxed shopping experience.

b. Sales and Discounts: Keep an eye out for seasonal sales and promotions, particularly during major holidays and the end of the summer season.

c. Local Recommendations: Don't hesitate to engage with the friendly locals and boutique owners who can offer personalized shopping recommendations and hidden gems.

d. Spa and Relaxation: After a day of shopping, indulge in the city's renowned spas and wellness centers to unwind and rejuvenate. Treat yourself to a relaxing massage or enjoy a luxurious spa treatment to complete your Palm Springs experience.

Palm Springs is a shopper's paradise and a fashion haven, offering a unique blend of modern trends, vintage treasures, and desert-inspired chic. With its diverse shopping districts, fashion events, and distinct fashion style, Palm Springs caters to every fashion enthusiast. Immerse yourself in the city's vibrant atmosphere, embrace the desert chic fashion, and discover hidden gems that will elevate your wardrobe.

Desert Resorts and Spas

Known for its year-round sunshine, stunning landscapes, and a rich cultural heritage, Palm Springs is an idyllic destination for those seeking relaxation, rejuvenation, and indulgence. Here, we invite you to explore the world of desert resorts and spas in Palm Springs, where you can immerse yourself in opulence, wellness, and natural beauty.

Unveiling the Oasis of Serenity
Palm Springs boasts an impressive collection of desert resorts and spas that are renowned for their exceptional service, breathtaking surroundings, and world-class amenities. These

199

luxurious retreats combine the natural beauty of the desert with meticulous attention to detail, offering guests an unparalleled experience of comfort and relaxation.

Desert Paradise: Captivating Resorts

When it comes to desert resorts, Palm Springs offers a range of options to suit every taste and preference. From lavish 5-star resorts to boutique hideaways, there's something for everyone. These resorts boast stunning architecture, lush gardens, and breathtaking mountain views, creating a serene atmosphere that transports you to a world of luxury and tranquility.

Immerse yourself in opulent accommodations, featuring spacious suites, private villas, and exquisite amenities. Indulge in fine dining experiences at award-winning restaurants, where renowned chefs blend international flavors with local ingredients. Unwind by pristine pools, surrounded by lush palm trees and the panoramic beauty of the desert landscape.

Wellness Oasis: Rejuvenating Spas

Palm Springs is also home to world-class spas that provide a haven for relaxation, healing, and well-being. The desert's natural energy and serene ambiance provide the perfect backdrop for indulging in rejuvenating treatments and therapies. From ancient healing traditions to innovative wellness programs, these spas offer a wide range of options to invigorate your mind, body, and soul.

Pamper yourself with soothing massages, revitalizing facials, and therapeutic body treatments that utilize organic, locally sourced ingredients. Experience the healing properties of natural hot springs and mineral-rich pools, renowned for their rejuvenating effects. Immerse yourself in yoga and meditation classes led by expert instructors, or take part in wellness workshops that promote holistic living.

Adventure in the Desert

While relaxation is paramount in Palm Springs, the region also offers a myriad of outdoor activities for the adventurous soul. Embark on guided hikes through the picturesque canyons of Joshua Tree National Park, exploring the unique flora and fauna of the desert. Engage in exhilarating outdoor pursuits such as hot air ballooning, horseback riding, or jeep tours, where you can witness stunning sunsets and panoramic vistas.

Beyond the resort and spa experiences, Palm Springs beckons with a vibrant cultural scene. Explore world-class art galleries, visit iconic mid-century modern architecture, or attend film festivals and live performances. Indulge in upscale shopping at designer boutiques, or unwind at golf courses nestled against the backdrop of the majestic San Jacinto Mountains.

Palm Springs, with its desert resorts and spas, invites you to embark on a journey of rejuvenation, indulgence, and serenity. Immerse yourself in the lap of luxury, where opulent accommodations, exquisite dining, and world-class spas ensure an unforgettable experience. With a wealth of outdoor activities and a vibrant cultural scene, Palm Springs offers a truly unique and captivating destination for those seeking a desert oasis. Plan your escape to this desert paradise, and let Palm Springs redefine the art of relaxation.

Chapter 7: Other destinations in Southern California

Santa Barbara

Santa Barbara stands as a true gem that effortlessly blends breathtaking natural beauty, rich cultural heritage, and a laid-back coastal lifestyle. Known as the "American Riviera," this captivating city entices visitors with its idyllic beaches, stunning Spanish architecture, thriving arts scene, and world-class vineyards. Join us as we embark on a journey through the enchanting charms of Santa Barbara, a destination that offers an irresistible blend of relaxation, adventure, and sophistication.

A Coastal Paradise

Santa Barbara boasts a coastline that stretches for 100 miles, with its golden sandy beaches caressed by the sparkling waters of the Pacific Ocean. The city is blessed with a Mediterranean climate, characterized by mild winters, sun-drenched summers, and a refreshing sea breeze. Popular beaches like East Beach, Butterfly Beach, and Leadbetter Beach provide the perfect settings for sunbathing, swimming, or indulging in a game of beach volleyball.

Spanish-Inspired Architecture

One of Santa Barbara's most captivating features is its architecture, heavily influenced by Spanish colonial heritage. Walking through the city's streets feels like stepping into a Mediterranean paradise, with its whitewashed buildings adorned with red-tile roofs, arched doorways, and charming courtyards. Don't miss a visit to the iconic Santa Barbara County Courthouse, a magnificent Spanish-Moorish structure that offers panoramic views of the city from its clock tower.

Cultural Haven

Santa Barbara's cultural scene is as vibrant as it is diverse. The city is home to numerous art galleries, museums, theaters, and music venues, showcasing a wide range of artistic expressions. The Santa Barbara Museum of Art houses a remarkable collection of European, American, and Asian art, while the Santa Barbara Bowl hosts world-class musical performances in a breathtaking outdoor amphitheater. Every summer, the Old Spanish Days Fiesta celebrates the region's heritage with colorful parades, dance performances, and delicious food.

Wine Country Paradise

Santa Barbara's fertile valleys and rolling hills provide the ideal conditions for growing grapes, making it a paradise for wine enthusiasts. The

Santa Ynez Valley, located just a short drive away, boasts an array of vineyards and wineries that produce exceptional wines. Take a leisurely drive along the Santa Barbara Wine Country Loop and indulge in wine tastings at renowned wineries such as Sanford Winery, Fess Parker Winery, and Bridlewood Estate Winery. Immerse yourself in the breathtaking vineyard landscapes and savor the flavors of the region.

Outdoor Adventures

Beyond its cultural and architectural wonders, Santa Barbara offers a plethora of outdoor activities for nature lovers and adventure seekers. Lace up your hiking boots and explore the stunning trails of the Los Padres National Forest or hike up to the iconic Inspiration Point for panoramic views of the city and coastline. For water enthusiasts, sailing, kayaking, and paddleboarding along the coast provide unforgettable experiences. The Channel Islands National Park, just off the coast, is a haven for wildlife, offering opportunities for snorkeling, diving, and encounters with seals and dolphins.

Santa Barbara effortlessly captures the essence of Southern California's coastal charm, with its breathtaking landscapes, cultural richness, and laid-back elegance. Whether you're seeking a relaxing beach getaway, a journey through history and art, or an outdoor adventure, this enchanting city has something for everyone. Explore its sun-kissed beaches, immerse yourself in its vibrant culture, and savor the flavors of its renowned wine country. Santa Barbara beckons you to embrace its captivating charms and create memories that will last a lifetime.

Catalina Island

Catalina Island stands as a captivating gem in the Pacific Ocean. Known for its breathtaking natural beauty, rich history, and abundant recreational activities, this enchanting island offers an idyllic escape from the bustling mainland. From rugged landscapes to pristine beaches and a myriad of outdoor adventures, Catalina Island promises an unforgettable experience for all who visit.

Natural Beauty

Catalina Island boasts a diverse landscape that spans over 76 square miles. With its towering cliffs, secluded coves, and lush hillsides, the island is a haven for nature enthusiasts. The dramatic backdrop of the Santa Catalina Mountains, with peaks reaching over 2,000 feet, offers breathtaking panoramic views of the Pacific Ocean. Exploring the island's extensive network of hiking trails rewards visitors with glimpses of stunning vistas, hidden valleys, and a plethora of endemic flora and fauna.

Avalon: Charming Harbor Town

The picturesque town of Avalon, Catalina Island's main hub, is a captivating blend of history and modern-day charm. The town's vibrant waterfront is adorned with colorful buildings, boutique shops, and cozy cafes, creating a delightful atmosphere for leisurely strolls. The iconic Casino Building, an architectural marvel, stands as a symbol of the island's golden age. Take a tour to discover its fascinating history and enjoy the breathtaking views from its observation deck.

Adventurous Water Activities

Catalina Island offers a treasure trove of water-based activities that cater to both thrill-seekers and those seeking relaxation. The crystal-clear waters surrounding the island are ideal for snorkeling and diving, revealing a vibrant marine ecosystem teeming with colorful fish, playful sea lions, and even the occasional dolphin sighting. Embark on a kayak or stand-up paddleboarding excursion to explore hidden coves and sea caves, or set sail on a boat tour to witness the majestic beauty of migrating whales.

Wildlife Encounters

Nature lovers will be delighted by the abundant wildlife that calls Catalina Island home. The Catalina Island Conservancy has played a vital role in preserving the island's natural habitats, allowing for encounters with unique species. The Catalina Island fox, found nowhere else on Earth, gracefully roams the island's interior. Bald eagles, a symbol of American resilience, have made a remarkable comeback and can be spotted soaring overhead. A visit to the island's Nature

Center provides an opportunity to learn more about these fascinating creatures.

Outdoor Pursuits

For those seeking an adrenaline rush, Catalina Island offers an array of outdoor activities. Experience the thrill of zip-lining through scenic canyons, reaching speeds of up to 30 miles per hour while taking in breathtaking vistas. Satisfy your adventurous spirit with a Jeep Eco-Tour, exploring the rugged terrain and hidden trails that unveil the island's raw beauty. Golf enthusiasts can enjoy a round of golf at the Catalina Island Golf Course, known for its stunning views and challenging fairways.

Catalina Island is a captivating paradise just a short ferry or helicopter ride away from the mainland. With its unparalleled natural beauty, charming harbor town, and abundance of outdoor activities, it offers a perfect blend of relaxation and adventure. Whether you're seeking a romantic getaway, a family vacation, or an outdoor enthusiast's haven, Catalina Island is a must-visit destination that promises an unforgettable experience for all who step foot on its shores.

Big Bear Lake

Big Bear Lake stands as an alluring oasis that captivates visitors with its breathtaking natural beauty and abundant recreational opportunities. Boasting a rich tapestry of stunning landscapes, thrilling outdoor adventures, and a charming alpine village, Big Bear Lake is a destination that beckons adventurers, nature lovers, and relaxation seekers alike. Join me as we embark on a journey to discover the wonders of this picturesque gem tucked away in the heart of Southern California.

Natural Splendor

Big Bear Lake is a scenic wonderland, offering an awe-inspiring natural landscape that enchants visitors throughout the year. The centerpiece of this picturesque destination is, of course, the eponymous Big Bear Lake itself. Spanning over 7 miles long and with a shoreline stretching for more than 22 miles, the lake is a haven for water enthusiasts. Its crystal-clear waters reflect the surrounding mountain peaks, creating a postcard-perfect panorama that is as calming as it is captivating.

Outdoor Adventures

Whether you seek pulse-pounding thrills or serene moments of tranquility, Big Bear Lake delivers an abundance of outdoor activities for all ages and interests. The region is renowned for its skiing and snowboarding opportunities during winter, with the Bear Mountain and Snow Summit resorts catering to enthusiasts of all skill levels. In the warmer months, the lake becomes a playground for water sports such as kayaking, paddleboarding, and fishing. Hiking and mountain biking trails weave through the surrounding forests, offering breathtaking vistas and opportunities to spot native wildlife.

Alpine Village Charm

Beyond the natural wonders, Big Bear Lake boasts a delightful alpine village that exudes a warm and inviting atmosphere. The village is brimming with quaint shops, boutiques, and galleries, where you can browse for unique treasures and souvenirs. Savor a diverse array of dining options, ranging from cozy cafes to gourmet restaurants, serving up everything from hearty mountain fare to international cuisines. The village also hosts various events and festivals throughout the year, creating a vibrant and festive ambiance that further enhances the visitor experience.

Four Seasons of Delight

Big Bear Lake is a year-round destination that showcases its beauty across all seasons. In the spring, witness the awakening of nature as wildflowers bloom and the surrounding mountains come alive with vibrant hues. The summer brings warm sunshine and a myriad of water activities, while fall graces the landscape with a stunning tapestry of golden foliage. Winter transforms Big Bear Lake into a winter wonderland, where snow-capped peaks and glistening ice create a truly magical setting for winter sports and cozy cabin retreats.

Escape and Relaxation

In addition to the exhilarating adventures and scenic wonders, Big Bear Lake offers a serene retreat from the fast pace of daily life. The tranquil atmosphere of the mountains, the calming presence of the lake, and the fresh alpine air combine to create an environment perfect for rejuvenation and relaxation. Whether you choose to unwind in a luxurious lakeside resort, cozy cabin, or charming bed and breakfast, Big Bear Lake offers a range of accommodations to suit every preference and budget.

Big Bear Lake stands as a true gem of Southern California, captivating visitors with its unparalleled natural beauty, abundant outdoor adventures, and charming alpine village. It is a destination that offers something for everyone, from thrilling sports enthusiasts to those seeking solace and relaxation amidst stunning landscapes. Embrace the allure of this enchanting oasis, and let Big Bear Lake create memories that will last a lifetime.

Temecula Valley Wine Country

With its rich history, warm Mediterranean climate, and award-winning wines, Temecula Valley is a must-visit destination for wine enthusiasts and nature lovers alike.

A Picturesque Landscape

As you approach Temecula Valley, you'll be greeted by a mesmerizing vista of undulating hills and lush vineyards as far as the eye can see. The region's unique geography, nestled between coastal mountains and the Pacific Ocean, creates an ideal microclimate for grape cultivation. The warm days and cool nights, coupled with the refreshing ocean breeze, bestow upon the grapes their distinctive flavors and aromas.

Vineyards and Wineries

Temecula Valley boasts over 40 wineries, each offering a unique experience and a taste of their exceptional wines. From small family-owned vineyards to grand estates, there is a winery to suit every palate. Explore the sun-kissed vineyards, wander through the rows of vines, and witness the meticulous craftsmanship that goes into producing each bottle.

Engage in wine tastings guided by passionate sommeliers, who will take you on an immersive journey through the region's diverse varietals. Whether you prefer robust reds, crisp whites, or delicate rosés, Temecula Valley has an impressive selection to please any wine lover. Don't miss the opportunity to savor the region's signature varietals, such as Cabernet Sauvignon, Syrah, Zinfandel, and Sauvignon Blanc.

Culinary Delights

The Temecula Valley Wine Country isn't just about wine; it's also a haven for food enthusiasts. Many wineries offer delightful food pairings, allowing you to indulge in a harmonious marriage of flavors. Immerse yourself in farm-to-table experiences, as many wineries grow their own produce or source it locally. Savor gourmet dishes meticulously crafted to complement the wines, elevating your taste buds to new heights.

Additionally, the region boasts an array of charming bistros, upscale restaurants, and al fresco dining options. Temecula Valley's culinary scene showcases the finest local ingredients, with a focus on seasonal and artisanal creations. Treat yourself to mouthwatering dishes prepared by talented chefs, and let the flavors of the valley dance on your palate.

Outdoor Adventures
Beyond its vineyards and wineries, Temecula Valley offers a host of outdoor activities and

natural wonders to explore. Embark on a hot air balloon ride and witness the valley's beauty from a bird's-eye perspective. As you float gently above the rolling hills, you'll be captivated by the patchwork of vineyards and the panoramic vistas stretching into the horizon.

For nature lovers, hiking and biking trails abound, allowing you to immerse yourself in the region's stunning landscapes. Discover hidden gems like the Santa Rosa Plateau Ecological Reserve, where you can witness diverse wildlife, unique flora, and stunning vistas. Enjoy a leisurely picnic amidst the beauty of nature, surrounded by the serenity of the valley.

Festivals and Events

Temecula Valley comes alive with a vibrant calendar of events throughout the year. Experience the magic of the annual Temecula Valley Balloon & Wine Festival, where hot air balloons fill the sky, and the valley celebrates its world-class wines. Indulge in wine tastings, live music, culinary delights, and thrilling balloon rides, creating memories that will last a lifetime.

The region also hosts the Temecula Valley International Film Festival, showcasing the artistry of talented filmmakers from around the world. Immerse yourself in the world of cinema, attend screenings, and engage in thought-provoking discussions with industry professionals.

Throughout the year, you'll find a variety of themed events and festivals celebrating the region's wine, food, music, and arts. From wine and food pairings to live concerts and art exhibitions, there's always something happening in Temecula Valley to pique your interest and provide an unforgettable experience.

Accommodations and Hospitality

Temecula Valley offers a range of accommodations, from cozy bed and breakfasts to luxurious resorts. Stay amidst the vineyards and wake up to breathtaking views of the sunrise over the rolling hills. Many wineries offer boutique accommodations, allowing you to fully immerse yourself in the wine country experience.

The hospitality of the locals is unmatched, with friendly vintners and winemakers eager to share their passion and knowledge. You'll feel welcomed as you explore the wineries, and the staff will be delighted to guide you through tastings and provide insights into the winemaking process. The warm and inviting atmosphere of Temecula Valley will make you feel like a part of the community.

Accessibility

Temecula Valley is conveniently located in Southern California, making it easily accessible from major cities such as Los Angeles, San Diego, and Palm Springs. It's an ideal day trip or weekend getaway for locals and a must-visit destination for tourists seeking an authentic wine country experience.

Whether you're a wine aficionado, a nature lover, or simply someone in search of a tranquil escape, Temecula Valley Wine Country has something for everyone. Indulge in the flavors of exceptional wines, delight in gourmet cuisine, immerse yourself in nature's beauty, and create memories that will last a lifetime.

Chapter 8: Practical Information for Visitors

Useful Phrases and Local slangs

One of the best ways to experience South California is to learn a few of the local phrases and slang terms. This will help you connect with the locals and make the most of your trip.

Here are a few useful phrases and local slang terms that you should know if you're planning a trip to South California:

Hella: This is a common way to say "very" or "a lot." For example, you might say, "That's hella cool!"

Gnarly: This means "awesome" or "great." For example, you might say, "That surf was gnarly!"

Rad: This is another way to say "awesome." For example, you might say, "That car is rad!"

Fo sho: This means "for sure." For example, you might say, "I'm going to the beach fo sho!"

Brah: This is a term of endearment that is often used between friends. For example, you might say, "What's up, brah?"

Dude: This is another term of endearment that is often used between friends. For example, you might say, "Hey dude, what's up?"

No worries: This means "don't worry about it." For example, you might say, "No worries, I got it covered."

Later: This means "goodbye." For example, you might say, "Later, dudes!"

Peace out: This is another way to say "goodbye." For example, you might say, "Peace out, brah!"

These are just a few of the many useful phrases and local slang terms that you should know if you're planning a trip to South California. By learning a few of these terms, you'll be able to connect with the locals and make the most of your trip.

It's also helpful to be aware of some of the cultural differences between South California and other parts of the world. For example, in South California, it's common to greet people with a hug or a kiss on the cheek. It's also considered rude to be too direct or assertive.

By being aware of these cultural differences, you can avoid any awkward moments and make the most of your trip to South California.

Cultural Do's and Dont's

From the bustling streets of Los Angeles to the laid-back beaches of San Diego, there is something for everyone to enjoy. Here are some cultural do's and don'ts to help you make the most of your trip:

Do's

- Explore different cultures. South California is home to people from all over the world, so be sure to take some time to explore the different cultures. Visit a local museum or cultural center, or simply strike up a conversation with someone from a different background.

- Be respectful of the environment. South California is a beautiful place, so be sure to do your part to protect it. Recycle, pick up your trash, and leave no trace.

- Try the local food. South California is home to some of the best food in the world, so be sure to try some of the local favorites. From tacos and burritos to sushi and seafood, there is something for everyone to enjoy.

- Be prepared for the heat. South California can be very hot, so be sure to pack light clothing, sunscreen, and a hat.

Don't's

- Don't drive like a maniac. Traffic in South California can be very congested, so be sure to drive safely and obey the speed limit.

- Don't be afraid to ask for directions. The people of South California are generally very friendly and helpful, so don't be afraid to ask for directions if you get lost.

- Don't be afraid to try new things. South California is a melting pot of cultures, so be sure to step outside of your comfort zone and try new things. You might just find something new that you love.

- Don't forget to relax and have fun. South California is a beautiful place, so be sure to relax and enjoy your time there. Take some time to soak up the sun, go for a swim, or simply wander around and explore.

I hope these do's and don'ts help you make the most of your trip to South California. Have a great time.

Emergency Services

In the vast and diverse region of Southern California, a dedicated group of individuals work tirelessly to keep its residents safe in times of crisis. From raging wildfires to devastating earthquakes and everything in between, the emergency services in Southern California stand as a beacon of hope and protection..

Fire Department
Southern California is no stranger to wildfires, which often pose a significant threat to life and property. The brave men and women of the local fire departments are always prepared to respond

swiftly and effectively. Equipped with state-of-the-art firefighting equipment, they battle flames, protect communities, and evacuate residents when necessary. Their commitment to safeguarding lives and minimizing the destruction caused by wildfires is truly awe-inspiring.

Law Enforcement

Maintaining law and order in a sprawling region like Southern California is an immense task, but the law enforcement agencies in the area rise to the occasion every day. Police officers diligently patrol the streets, responding to emergencies, preventing crime, and ensuring public safety. Their professionalism and dedication serve as a constant reminder that Southern California is a place where people can feel secure and protected.

Emergency Medical Services

Accidents and medical emergencies can strike at any time, and Southern California's emergency medical services (EMS) teams are always prepared to respond swiftly. Paramedics and emergency medical technicians (EMTs) provide life-saving care on the frontlines, stabilizing patients and transporting them to hospitals. Their ability to remain calm under pressure and make split-second decisions often makes the difference between life and death. The EMS teams of Southern California embody the spirit of compassion and resilience in the face of adversity.

Search and Rescue

Southern California's diverse terrain, including mountains, deserts, and coastal areas, presents unique challenges when it comes to search and rescue operations. Whether it's hikers stranded in remote areas, lost individuals, or victims of natural disasters, highly trained search and rescue teams risk their own safety to save others. Armed with specialized skills, equipment, and unwavering determination, they locate and extricate individuals in distress, providing a lifeline when hope seems lost.

Emergency Management

The key to effectively handling emergencies lies in preparedness and coordination. Emergency management agencies in Southern California work tirelessly behind the scenes to develop comprehensive plans, conduct drills, and coordinate resources. These professionals ensure that communication flows seamlessly among various emergency services, government entities, and the public. Their proactive approach enables a swift and well-coordinated response when disaster strikes.

The emergency services in Southern California are a shining example of courage, selflessness, and resilience. Their dedication to protecting lives, preserving property, and maintaining order in the face of adversity is truly commendable. As residents of this vibrant region, we owe a debt of gratitude to these unsung heroes who stand ready to answer the call of duty at a moment's notice. Their tireless efforts remind us that, even in the darkest times, there are individuals who embody the spirit of service and remain unwavering in their commitment to safeguarding our community.

Conclusion

As we bring our epic South California travel guide to a close, we can't help but feel a tinge of bittersweet nostalgia. Our adventure through this remarkable region has been an extraordinary tapestry of vibrant experiences, breathtaking landscapes, and an unparalleled fusion of cultures. From the sun-drenched beaches of San Diego to the star-studded streets of Los Angeles, from the awe-inspiring natural wonders of Joshua Tree National Park to the iconic glamour of Palm Springs, South California has left an indelible mark on our hearts and minds.

Throughout our journey, we have unraveled the diverse and dynamic spirit that defines this part of the Golden State. South California embodies a unique blend of laid-back coastal vibes, bustling urban energy, and a commitment to preserving its natural wonders. The region beckons travelers with its promises of sun-soaked adventures, cultural immersion, and opportunities for self-discovery.

Our exploration of the coast revealed a captivating world where soft sand meets the crashing waves of the Pacific Ocean. Whether it was surfing the legendary breaks of Malibu, strolling along the Santa Monica Pier, or indulging in the vibrant beach culture of Huntington Beach, the coastal cities of South California showcased a lifestyle that celebrates the great outdoors. The captivating sunsets that painted the sky with hues of gold and purple provided the perfect backdrop for moments of reflection and awe.

As we ventured inland, the landscapes transformed into a kaleidoscope of natural wonders. Joshua Tree National Park, with its otherworldly rock formations and enchanting Joshua trees, reminded us of the captivating beauty of the desert. The park's hiking trails led us to hidden oases, where we reveled in the serenity of the desert's silence. Big Bear Lake, nestled in the San Bernardino Mountains, provided an idyllic escape for outdoor enthusiasts, with its pristine waters, scenic hikes, and thrilling winter sports.

No visit to South California would be complete without exploring the vibrant metropolis of Los Angeles. This sprawling city is a cultural melting pot, where dreams are born and realized. From the glitz and glamour of Hollywood to the artistic enclaves of Silver Lake and Venice Beach, Los Angeles embodies the essence of creativity and aspiration. We walked in the footsteps of stars along the Hollywood Walk of Fame, indulged in world-class cuisine, and experienced the thrill of live performances in iconic venues like the Hollywood Bowl.

Palm Springs, with its retro charm and Mid-Century Modern architecture, transported us to a bygone era of Hollywood glamour. We relaxed in luxurious spas, played a round of golf against a backdrop of majestic mountains, and explored the city's renowned collection of vintage boutiques and art galleries. The desert oasis offered us a respite from the hustle and bustle of city life, allowing us to unwind and reconnect with ourselves.

Throughout our South California odyssey, we also delved into the region's rich cultural tapestry. The diverse communities that call this place home have infused it with a vibrant energy and a wealth of traditions. From the authentic Mexican cuisine of San Diego's Old Town to the colorful celebrations of Dia de los Muertos in Santa Ana, we were treated to a plethora of cultural delights. We marveled at the Getty Center's world-class art collection, wandered through the historic streets of Old Pasadena, and got lost in the maze-like streets of Little Tokyo, immersing ourselves in the flavors and colors of different cultures.

As we bid farewell to South California, we carry with us a lifetime of memories, a deeper understanding of the region's unique character, and a longing to return. The experiences we shared, the sights we beheld, and the people we met have shaped our perception of this remarkable place. South California is a destination that promises endless possibilities.

Printed in Great Britain
by Amazon

23110254R00136